THE BIG B
Funny Yorkshire

Dalesman

First published in Great Britain in 2014 by Dalesman Publishing
an imprint of
Country Publications Ltd
The Water Mill, Broughton Hall
Skipton, North Yorkshire BD23 3AG

ISBN 978-1-85568-336-5

Printed in China on behalf of Latitude Press Ltd.

Introduction

WE MAY inhabit England's biggest and most diverse county but one thing that unites Yorkshire folk is our sense of humour. From the big cities of Leeds and Bradford to the sparsely populated rolling hills of the Yorkshire Dales, Tykes love to crack a joke.

While wry smiles may be preferred over gales of laughter, the people of Yorkshire will make light of the darkest of subjects with a unique brand of self-deprecating wit. A Yorkshireman will not hesitate to poke fun at himself, his family, friends or even the home county he is so proud of. Nor does he mind if he is the subject of the joke – though he will always give as good as he takes.

The bluntest of Yorkshire humour can be attributed to the county's tough industrial and farming heritage, and its decidedly temperamental climate. But while, as a result, Yorkshire humour tends to be direct and frill-free it is, as a rule, pretty clean and is often rather sophisticated. There is much wisdom, as well as wit, to be found in the humour of the Broad Acres.

For the last seventy-five years, *Dalesman* magazine has been collecting hundreds of these jokes, tall tales and anecdotes from across the three Ridings. And in this new collection, taken directly from the magazine's archives, we have selected the cream of the crop. In the pages that follow you'll find hundreds of jokes on just about every topic imaginable, which all go to prove just how funny Yorkshire can be.

Adrian Braddy, Dalesman *editor*

Gerrin' Up!

Ah hate gerrin' up
On a mornin' for school;
Ah'd reyther lig in
Aw! Ah might be a fooil.

Ah allus feel sleepy;
Ah'm idle the' say.
Well, happen Ah am
At that time o' t' day!

Ah'm noddin', an' drowsy;
Ah hear 'em shaht "Fred!"
But Ah snuggle dahn
A bit farther i' bed.

Me mutther says "Gow!
Tha fairly tak's t' caik.
it's holiday-time.
Nay! Gerrup an' laik."

Will Clemence

A DALESWOMAN'S view of her teenage daughter: "Oo 'er shill nivver mek an 'ousewife. She nobbut sweeps a room wi a glance."

OVERHEARD in a Halifax pub. A man raised his glass and said, "Cheers to all weavers' wives. They all knaw t' worst abaht us but they still wain't believe it."

Overheard in Selby market. "Ah don't like these quiet chaps 'at say nowt. Mi father telt me that its t' quietest pig wot eats most food in t' trough."

A BOY in a Dales village was asked by his pal to go catching eels in the beck.

"Nah, Ah can't go wi thi. Ah's got to stay yam to 'elp me dad do mi homework."

> *A trout eats well;*
> *A beck laughs loud*
> *A wheel works well;*
> *And wool wears well*
> *And so does a Yorkshireman!*

THERE is an old Dales saying: if you want to do a man a bad turn, leave 'im an old cottage in yer will.

DAVID Turton (1768-1846) of Horbury, near Wakefield, who rests in the churchyard of his native place, was a musician of no mean parts. One amazing episode is that of his routing of an oncoming bull in a field, when he 'unbagged' his bass viol and played the very note of the animal's bellow which he decided was 'double B flat', and with such decisive effect that the animal turned tail. David then treated his foe to a Handel chorus.

A Gypsy bargaining for a horse with an old dales farmer: "I'm not askin' fer its pedigree or whether it's got any vices. I'm tekking yon animal as if it were a wife."

A NEW groom speaking at his wedding breakfast in Bradford made a short speech but very much to the point: "My new missus is just reet. If she'd bin any better I wouldna 'ev git her, an' if she'd bin any worse I wouldna 'ave 'ad 'er. So ah reckons she's just reet."

T' Lass I'm Bahn to Wed

Mi mother she's inquisitive.
"Who're ta cooarting lad?" she said.
"Come on nahr, I know it's reight,
Who's t' lass tha bahn to wed?"

At this I turned mi head away.
Mi face went blazing red.
I hum'd an' ah'd, then aht it came.
"It's Jessie Weatherhead."

"Yond lass!" she looked an' sahnded capped,
"'At works in t' weaving shed,
Spends all she addles on her back,
An' paints her fingers red?

"She'll ne-er know ahr to mend thi clooas,
Wesh, bake and mak a bed."
"Well nivver heed, if she suits me,
That's all 'at cahnts" I said.

"She's worsted warp an' woollen weft,
Worked through wi' silken thread.
And woven on five shuttles,
Wor Jessie Weatherhead.

"Straight as a picking-rod is Jess.
Wi' pride she holds her head.
Nowt shall tak' mi' hear away
Thru t' lass I'm bahn to wed."

George Taylor

A DALESWOMAN near Kettlewell had her views on the Second World War when she said: "Well blitz or no blitz we've 'ad such grand weather. It's bin one o' them days wot I love. Cotton-wool clouds throwing shadows on t' moor tops and t' birds singin' their little 'arts aht. I thowt, poor lile Hitler. 'Ee thinks ee's going to hev t' last word but our birds'll be singing long after his wickedness is done wi'."

A SALESMAN knew that an old woman from Nidderdale was having trouble walking. He was doing his best to sell her husband a stairlift and got this reply.

"We's git yan. I just go up on t' landin' and pull aht t' weights on yon grandfather clock. I gits 'em dahn stairs and puts 'em in t' wife's 'ands. Then I winds up t' clock and up she goes."

A four-year-old lad was travelling with his mother on a bus in Leeds when he saw a man with a bald patch on the back of his head. He shouted to his mum: "Look, Mam, yon man's gitten an 'ole in 'is 'air."

BLACK Lead Martha was a woman of opinion and character. Martha used to black lead her legs in summer to be cool and save her black stockings. This was before the days of suntan lotion. Martha also smoked a clay pipe, and drank cinder tea for wind.

A YOUNG couple had just left the family farm to set off on their honeymoon. The rest of the family were having a 'crack by the fireside' when one of the brothers, a father of five children and with another one 'hatching', told of how he had smuggled confetti into the luggage of the couple. The family was still laughing as the farmer went out to get on with the evening milking.

One of the five children piped up and said: "That's a reet good idea. I's goin' to do that when Daddy goes on 'is unnymoon."

STONE wallers were sometimes paid by the day rather than by the yard and a local farmer was annoyed when he found his waller sheltering from the rain.

"Nah then lad," he growled, "why is ter sheltering instead o' building?"

"Well boss – 'ow do you 'spect me to mek thee a dry stone wall when it's so wet?"

THERE was an old character in Keighley called 'Joe Pump'. He played a concertina and went round the streets busking, accompanied by 'Sally Matchbox' who sang while he played.

NOT ALL babies are born beautiful and a dalesman's wife presented him with his fifth son who was born wrinkled and not a pretty sight. The following morning he found his eldest son had been involved in a fight.

"Who's tha bin feeting this time?" he asked.

"I's bin belting up James Clarkson."

"Int 'e t' doctor's lad? Why did thi pick on 'im?"

"Cos his father's cheated on us. Yon baby he's palmed off on us is nobbut an old un."

SEEN on the gravestone of a Blacksmith:

My sledge and hammer have declined
My bellows too have lost their wind
My fire's extinct my forge decayed
And in the dust my vice is laid;
My coals are spent, my iron's gone
My nails are drove – my work is done
My fire-dryed corpse lies here at rest,
My soul, smoke-like, soars to be blest.

OVERHEARD on Whitby pier as two fishermen returned from a trip:

"Aye t' roak were so thick that if we 'adn't known where we wor we wudent 'a known where we wor."

'SALT JIM' of Bradford went round the streets selling two-foot-long blocks of salt. He used a two-wheeled flat cart drawn by a donkey. Jim called on business houses and offices knowing full well they would not buy his salt but hoping for a tip instead. He called out: "Salt, salt, want any salt? Come on it's bahn to snow."

Occasionally he would walk in front of the donkey. It would plant its front feet on Jim's shoulders and bray loudly.

SPRING Heel Jack of Whitby was a born vagabond. He got his name from his mode of travel. He used a contraption like a short stout walking stick, with a second handle about six inches from the top. Grasping it with both hands, he would give a spring and a bound covering the ground at a great pace.

He called at various places to eat his meagre lunch which was a big chunk of bread and a raw onion. He then rested for a while, spat on his hands, grasped his propeller and set off like the wind.

A DALESMAN who was useless in the kitchen had to fend for himself when his wife went off to look after her sick father. One of his friends gave him some rhubarb and told him how to make a pie. When the friend called the day after he saw a pie on the table which was three feet long.

"Wot's tha doin' wi yon pie?" he asked.

"It's thy fault – tha should 'a gi' mi shorter lumps."

EPITAPH for a plough:

> *Yes an old wooden plow and they say to be sure*
> *The wide-awake farmer must use them no more*
> *They must be of iron, for wood there's no trade for.*
> *What do the fools think God made these ash trees for?*

THE EDITOR of a Yorkshire newspaper decided to write the report of his own wedding. Instead of describing the bride's wedding dress he wrote as follows: "The groom wore a bluish business suit, recently cleaned and pressed. The coat fitted snugly across the back with lapels on either side at the front. Beneath the coat and waistcoat was a freshly laundered white shirt across which lay a grey and blue tie. The groom also wore shoes, polished. The laces were tied in small bows."

A WORKER on the counter of a post office told of the time when a half-crown book of stamps was first introduced and there were blanks left where the space did not tally with the price. An old daleswoman asked for one and said, "An' I want a full book this time. Last time tha give me a book wi' three blanks in it but I used all t' same."

DURING a spell of bad weather a Daleswoman decided to take her children's mid-day meal up to the school to save them the trouble of trudging home in the snow. A little later they arrived home and burst into the house. The dishes had been washed. "Here you are, mum. We knew you didn't like leaving dirty pots."

A north countryman and a south countryman were each boasting about their own part of the country. The Londoner said: "If you want to see the cup final you have to come to London."

The northerner's reply: "Ay an' if tha wants to see t' cup after t' final tha'll 'ave to come up north."

IN 1958 Yorkshire cricketer Vic Wilson had a benefit. The following day he wanted to say thank you to the crowd which raised £268. Vic bowed and raised his cap and waved it to all parts of the ground. A wag shouted:

"Ee's nobbut bein' greedy. Ee's not gitten enuff, ee's off rahnd wi' 'is cap nah."

A WOMAN in Bradford was buying her Sunday roast from the Co-op and asked the butcher to put in a big soup bone.

"That'll be four-and-tuppence please."

"How much did tha charge for yon soup bone?"

"Nowt," was the reply, "I've just thrown that in for thi."

"Nay tha wain't," the woman shouted, "tha's not doin' me out o' mi divvi – thee git it weighed."

A VERY rich gentleman was extremely angry when his train was late and he missed an important connection. He went up to the driver and shouted: "This is not good enough. I gave the guard a pound note to ensure the train ran on time."

"Is tha saying that thou gave guard a pahnd?"

"Yes I did."

"Well nah, all I kin say is that thou tipped wrong end o' t' train!"

A YOUNG man from London worked on the railway and was posted to Earby junction. On his first morning on duty when the main line train drew in he marched up and down the platform shouting, "All change for Barnolds ...wick."

Nobody got out and the stationmaster went up to him and said, "Ey up lad, tha's gittin' it wrong. Tha does it like this 'ere."

He then walked up and down the platform yelling at the top of his voice, "Swap trucks wi' Barlick – Swap trucks wi' Barlick."

There was a rush of passengers moving from the main line to the branch line train.

A dalesman's view of a lazy workman:
"Ee's like an owd pig's tail. Ee's weggin' all day and nowt's done at neet."

Yorkshire

Niver cum to Yorkshire
If tha doan't like muck
For there's coil pits all ower
Enough to fill a book
If tha doen't like Yorkshire puddin'
Tha'd better stop away,
'Cos when tha goes to some hoames
Tha gets it ivery day.

But there's miles an' miles of beauty
Of that tha may be sure;
There's many a ruined abbey
And castles by the score
We haven't got 'igh mountains
But we've many a luvely dale
And many a rushin' river
The Wharfe and Ure and Swale.

And if tha's wantin' ozone
There's plenty 'ere it's true
Although it's not 'Pacific'
The sea is often blue.
So think about this Yorkshire
Then p'raps tha'll cum and see
Which ever place tha comes from
There's a welcome 'ere for thee.

By fourteen-year-old Veronica Ward, Pontefract

KNOCK 'em Down Tommy was the nickname of an old dales preacher. He arrived at Redmire station and the porter looked at his face which reminded him of a pugilist.

"Art thee a fighter?" asked the porter.

"I am lad."

"Whose that fightin' here?"

"Well I's just come from fightin' in Dent, Settle and Skipton and I's goin' to fight right 'ere."

"Who art tha fightin'?"

"I thowt that tha would 'a known. I'm fightin' the devil and the demon drink all i' one day."

THERE was a curious regular at the bar of Gaiety Bar in Sheffield where the owner bought a pig to be fattened to provide a hog-roast for a gala night. He called the pig Lucy but got so fond of her that he could not kill her. Lucy developed a liking for a couple of pints of 'old and mild'. In the evening, during the interval of the music hall routine, Lucy would squeak to be let in. She would squeak again at the bar until two pints had been provided and then she would grunt, roll over and go to sleep. "She were more popular than any act I paid for," the landlord grinned.

A young lad from the dales told his teacher, "A cow is a ruminatin' hanimal cos it chews its own cubs. I 'ad a white mouse once that et five on 'em."

A VILLAGE felt that it needed a new village hall with the present meeting place just a wooden hut. A huge notice appeared on the hut.

"At the present time this HUT is your village hall. If you want a larger village hall you will have to help to build it. UMPTEEN LABOURERS WANTED. Rate of pay NOWT per hour. Plenty of overtime at double this rate. Apply to the site foreman whose rate of pay is 100% more than yours will be."

A YOUNG lad from Askham near York worked for a farmer named Swann. He was busy one day by the village pond feeding the ducks when he was approached by an American tourist.

"Are these ducks yours, son?" he asked.

"No, them's Swanns."

The American looked at the lad and asked, "Where do you come from?"

"Askham," replied the lad.

The American drove off tapping his head.

IT TAKES time for newcomers to be accepted in Dales villages. An elderly resident overheard a conversation in the local butcher's and described the new family as 'early settlers'.

"Eye up," said the dalesman, "yon lot have nobbut just cum, 'ow is it tha sez they be early settlers?"

"That's because they settle their bills long afore thee," was the reply.

TWO OLD daleswomen in a café were looking at a modern young lass wearing the shortest of mini-skirts. The girl sat down, crossed her legs and asked the waitress if she could close the window because of the draught. One old lady got up and said to the girl, "Nay, lass. If tha wore a decent frock tha'd nivver feel yon draught."

AN OLD farmer near Skipton was a bit of a hypochondriac and was always taking to his bed. A new doctor arrived and advised him to get out and about more in the good weather.

Two weeks later his wife reported him to be much better. Later she met the doctor in the street and he asked, "How's Jack?"

"Ee's very ill," said his wife.

"What's wrong with him?"

"Sunstroke I think," said the wife with a broad grin on her face.

IN THE days of the old-time music hall the manager was auditioning new acts. He looked at a young comedian and said, "Tha's no use ter me. We don't have any profanity in 'ere."

"But I don't use profanity," said the young hopeful.

"I know tha don't use it – but I's damn sure t' audience would."

A GARDENER in Wharfedale pointed out, "I's allus a gardener and an ornithologist. We both spends all our time feedin' yon wild birds."

A vicar's wife was upset that small boys were using bad language when playing marbles. She asked what would happen when they were older.

The reply was, "They grow up, play golf and use t' same words."

A DOCTOR in the Dales noticed that his door bell was not ringing and he placed a notice 'Out of Order' close to the push button. A fortnight later a farmer called in and asked the doctor if he was better.

"I've not been ill," replied the doctor.

"Well I cummed a couple of weeks back and tha 'ad a notice up saying tha were outer order and so I went 'oame."

A SOPRANO singing in a Dewsbury music hall was trying without much luck to hit a high note.

"I'll hang my harp on a weeping willow," she sang but missed the high note.

She tried once more before a voice from the back shouted, "Try hanging thi 'arp on a lower branch lass."

UNDER any other business a WI secretary announced details of the following week's speaker: "We'll be 'aving Mrs Jackson an' 'er concussion band."

A YOUNG lad was walking along the beach and asked his mother, "What's that sticking up?"

"It's a lighthouse."

"What's it for?"

"It is to stop ships always getting on the rocks."

"Shall we get one for Daddy?"

Overheard on the sands at Bridlington: "Ee, mother, if we'd only pawned t' other feather bed we could 'a stayed on 'ere over t' weekend."

A MOTHER sent her son to the butcher's. "Ax 'im fer a side view will ter?"

After he had understood what his mother meant, off he went. When the butcher asked what he meant the lad replied, "It's 'alf a pig's 'ead an' she wants it off one that's 'ad the toothache so there's more on it. An' don't tek eyes out on it so it'll see us through t' rest of t' week."

"Does ta want it wrapping up?"

"Aye, an' put a pahnd o' sausages wi' it."

A WOMAN entering a butcher's shop asked for a land surveyor. She was given a sheep's head.

Land Fever
(With apologies to John Masefield's 'Sea Fever')

I must go back to the land again
To the verdant fields and the soil,
For the products of my toil:
And the tractor's 'chug', and the thresher's hum,
And the even tread of the sower,
The fruitful rain, and the golden grain,
And the rattle of the mower.

I must go back to the land again,
To the fields of waving corn,
The hedgerows in the springtime,
With flowers and budding thorn;
The smell of the summer hayfield,
I must go back to the land again,
For the land is calling.

Ernest Harrison, Newton-in-Bowland

A DALESWOMAN was given a brace of grouse by the local squire and as she was cooking them she growled to her husband.

"Yon grouse is a fool of a bird – they be too much for yan to eat and not enuf for twa."

A VISITOR to the Dales said to an old lad, "Here there is beautiful clean air. People won't often die here will they?"

The reply came quickly. "Na, nobbut yance."

AN AMERICAN photographer on vacation was inside a church in Oldham taking photographs when he noticed a golden telephone mounted on the wall with a sign that read '£10,000 per call'.

The American, being intrigued, asked a priest who was strolling by what the telephone was used for. The priest replied that it was a direct line to Heaven and that for £10,000 you could talk to God. The American thanked the priest and went along his way.

Next stop was in Manchester. There, at a very large cathedral, he saw the same golden telephone with the same sign under it. He wondered if this was the same kind of telephone he saw in Oldham and he asked a nearby nun what its purpose was. She told him that it was a direct line to heaven and that for £10,000 he could talk to God.

"OK, thank you," said the American.

He then travelled to Blackburn, Darwen, Burnley, Rochdale and Littleborough. In every Lancashire church the price was £10,000 per call.

However, on reaching Skipton he discovered the cost of the call was only 10p. "Why is it so cheap here?" he asked.

The priest smiled and answered, "You're in Yorkshire now, son. It's nobbut a local call."

Can I have mi bull back?

ON A BRIGHT sunny day a man was passing through Hawes. He saw a farm lad pushing an empty wheelbarrow in and out of a barn.

"Wot's tha doin' lad?" he asked.

"T' hay were damp so I's tekking a bit o' sunshine in to it to dry it aht."

AN OLD gardener was working in his garden near Leyburn when a townie asked him the difference between a marrow and a pumpkin. He sniffed and replied, "A marrer is a marrer an' a pumpkin's a pumpkin and a cucumber is nowt like either on 'em."

BOB WAS a well-known Methodist local preacher. At a camp in Garsdale he started on his sermon. He'd selected a hillock for his pulpit and began his discourse in his customary vivacious manner, but he had not proceeded far before he halted, and, turning to the assembled brethren, said, "There's no doubt I've got the love of God in my heart, but, I think, I've got the Devil in my breeches!"

Bob had not only stirred the congregation before him, but had caused a commotion among the ants below him.

A Lass of Mi Own

I allus wanted a lass o' mi own
One wi' bonny brown hair.
But none of 'em ever smiled at me
To look at Ah'm nut very fair.

Then Meg passed mi by, wi' a look in 'er eye
But bi then mi courage had fled
Ah needn't 'ave feered, for good was 'er word
And 'appy the day we wuz wed".

Elizabeth Glennon

A DENTIST was once treating a high court judge. As he was preparing for an extraction the judge grinned and said, "Do you swear that you will pull out the tooth, the whole tooth and nothing but the tooth?"

VERY rarely Owd John the cobbler ventured out of his humble form of living and then it was only to return to it with many scathing remarks. Having once heard that some of the local gentry were eating cucumber, he purchased one which he cut up lengthwise into long strips with the skin still on.

These he put into his frying pan together with a liberal amount of dripping. After much sizzling it appeared to have arrived at the edible stage. Drawing his high-backed chair up to his table he commenced his meal and never made any comments until he had finished.

Then, after wiping the grease from his mouth with the back of his hand, he said, "Weel, they may be alreet for t' gentry fooak, but gi' me a taty onny time."

AN OLD daleswoman was looking closely into the window of an optician's. The assistant came out and asked if there was anything he could do.

The old lass looked at him and said, "Nah then lad, is it foggy today?"

"No Madam."

"Is there a fire then?"

"No Madam."

"Is yer sure it's not foggy?"

"Yes Madam, it's a lovely clear day."

"Reet then, I'll come in to see if there's summat wrong wi' mi eyes."

JOHNNY Clarke, the village sexton, had no love of chapel folk. One hot summer the vicar held prayers for rain, and still the drought continued, so he decided to call on the Nonconformist party for united effort. Johnny was sadly put out about calling in the 'ranters' and prophesied that no good would come of it.

That same night of united prayers, a terrific thunderstorm broke over the district, washing farmer Merril's turnips out of the hill field into the beck and doing lots of damage. Johnny saw the wreckage next morning and said: "It's them ranters! I knew how it 'ud be, fetchin' them ranters in, they allus overdo it."

"WE 'AD thi brother preachin' at t' chapel last Sunday," said one dalesman.

"Aye, and wor 'e any good? " asked the other.

"He wor a reet good un."

"An' what did 'e preach abaht?"

"Nay, Ah can't tell thee that, but he'd done an' we wor outside by awf-past-eleven."

A NATIVE of Swaledale once had occasion to travel farther up the dale, taking with him a young friend whom he had staying with him at that time. After his business was completed, his friend enquired of the dalesman whether there were any cafes in the village. Fixing his gaze on the hillside opposite, the dalesman answered "Just a minute."

The visitor also glanced across to the hillside, and saw a procession slowly wending its way downwards to the village. When the procession reached the village the dalesman joined on behind and the surprised visitor followed suit. It was a funeral procession.

The two went to the chapel and sat through the funeral service after which the undertaker announced that lunch would be provided at the village hotel for all friends from a distance.

When they got outside, the visitor asked the dalesman whose funeral it was, whereupon the dalesman promptly replied, "I don't know, but we've mourned wi' t' mourners so we'll feast wi' t' feasters."

"When I wor a lad we just had one sort – called muck."

A FARMER was complaining about a lazy young farm-hand who said: "I's tired boss. I'm reet snuffed aht."

"Snuffed aht?" growled the farmer, "tha's nivver ivver bin lit."

A MAN from Barnsley bought a secondhand motorcycle. He took it to a quiet country road for practice. Suddenly he was overtaken by a car which flew past at an amazing speed. The motorcyclist wobbled and then fell off.

He called in the nearest pub and there sat the driver of the car. He went up to the driver and asked him to pay for his muddy clothes caused by his fall.

"Nay," said the driver, "Ah nivver touched thi."

"Ah knows that," said the motorcyclist, "but the'll 'ev to pay. Tha whizzed past soa fast, ah thowt I'd stopped an' ah got off!"

A dalesman reporting events when a woman was taken ill with violent pains and hurried off to hospital: "They opun'd 'er up and fund an internal ablution, t' last we 'eard was they was givin' 'er a blood confusion."

A PHONE call to a dales police station reported that a farmer had been attacked outside his front door. The policeman returned soon after and said to his sergeant that he had solved the case.

"How did you do that so quick?"

"I stood on t' same rake," said the constable rubbing his jaw.

AN OLD dales farmer was fond of his cup of tea but it had to be poured out from an ancient brown teapot. One day his wife decided that the teapot was "too mucky" so she filled it up with washing soda and hot water and left it to soak.

The old man arrived home early and when his wife returned from feeding the chickens she was surprised to find him sipping tea.

"Ee lass," he said, "that were a reet grand brew. I had three cups afore I had to top it up wi' more watter."

In March we long for April
In May we long for June
Don't be in such a hurry
It will all be gone too soon.

AN ECCENTRIC walker was well known to the residents in Swaledale. One day he strode through the village of Crackpot waving a flag and two villagers watched him go. One said to the other, "Thee-er 'ee gahs. We've now gitten two Crackpots in our spot but yans faster than t' other!"

A COUPLE in Harrogate were expecting a visit from the local vicar. They knew that he always asked the same questions: the age of the child, the name and where naughty children went. The vicar arrived and asked the questions. The vicar was aghast at the reply:

"Five years old sir, Mary and go to hell!"

AT A WI class in Pateley Bridge a German lady was engaged to talk about her language to a class of dalesfolk.

"Tonight," said the lady, "vee vill talk about ein railvay journey. Ze German for station is der Bahnhof. Can anybody find a gut vay to remember der Bahnhof?"

"Ay lass, I can," said an old daleswoman. "Winivver Ah gahs to t' station Ah'm allus bahn off somewhere."

The whole class laughed and the poor German lady just looked confused.

> *Hills of the North Rejoice!*
> *There's pavin' stoans under thi feet lad*
> *Pavin' stoans cowd an' 'ard*
> *There's t' mill chimleys belchin' smoak lad*
> *O'er weshin' hangin' in t' yard.*
>
> *But there's green in t' hills rising up lad*
> *Risin' up o'er all this grime*
> *Trees an' t' fields full o' green lad*
> *The've bin 'ere since start o' time.*
>
> *Judy Worth*

AFTER A series of power cuts a notice appeared outside the Electricity Company's office in Bradford:

"The supply is working okay now. Only the person in charge needs changing."

OVERHEARD in a dales village hall at the end of a concert: "How did you enjoy the young soprano?" asked the chairman.

"She wuz luvely," replied a farmer's wife, "she 'ed a voice like a gramophone."

A TRAVELLING circus visited a Yorkshire town every year. One old chap noticed that an elephant was limping and so he removed a sharp stone from its foot. The next year the man was in the audience when one of the elephants raised its trunk and moved him from the shilling seats and into a half-a-crown seat!

A gardener's wife was astounded when she was told that her son had "etten three pounds o' new spuds" whilst she was out.

"How did you eat so much?" she gasped.

"It's a'reet Ma — they were nobbut little uns."

A FAMILY in Huddersfield were expecting a second baby and the father said to his five-year-old son, "The stork has been flying around our house lately."

He was interrupted by the lad who said, "Oh dear, Dad, I hope Mum isn't frightened by it. She's expecting a baby you know."

A DALESWOMAN brought up eight children, did the housework, fed the farmhands and helped with the farm work. She was asked how she managed all of this without having a break for almost thirty years.

"Aye, I've thowt of 'avin' a nervous breakdown but just as I was sittin' dahn to 'ave one it were time to get some on 'em a meal."

The Dredger

The thing I like most about Whitby
I think it's incredible luck,
Is an ancient and moribund dredger
Dredging buckets and buckets of mud.

And when it has filled up its hopper
With a beautiful puddle of black.
It takes it, and dumps it, outside the harbour
And the seas brings all of it back.

Pat Wilson

A CHILD'S view: "University is a kind o' collidge wot folk go to who aren't properly growed up."

A SMALL girl was putting her dolls to bed and was being watched by her mother.

"I'm sure, lass, that tha's a lot of bairns to care for."

"Aye Mum, and I'm expectin' agin at Crismaz."

THE SNOW had fallen thickly overnight. An old dalesman was asked what he thought of the weather:

"T' weather's not reet. Frost an' snow should cum in summer when t' weathers warm. Instead o' that it allus cums i' winter when t' weather is as cold as ice."

AN OLD dales farmer called into his local pub for a drink. It was freezing cold and he was soaked to the skin.

A stranger stood up and gave him his seat.

"Thankee, lad I's eighty-one."

"Thee keep goin', lad, and don't catch cold. I's ninety-three."

"You're right Sarge. Arresting crooks is one thing;
arresting sheep's another!"

A MAN walking by a dales river came across three men fishing a very wet youngster out of the water.

"Well done you three," he called, "you've saved the lad, is he related to one of you?"

"Nah, ee's not but he's gitten our bait in his pocket."

AN OVERLOOKER in a Halifax mill found a stray kitten under a pile of wool and took it home to his wife.

"Here thou is lass," he said, "I've browt thee a kittin."

The kitten bolted under the sofa, was hauled out only to shoot back again and continued to do this all evening.

"Ah'll cure t' lile devil. Thee git thissen off to bed lass an' I'll sort it aht."

When he finally came to bed his wife asked, "Has ta cured yon kittin?"

"Aye," said the overlooker. "Ah've sawed t' legs off t' sofa."

A LECTURER was giving a talk to a group of elderly daleswomen on the subject of England's greatest play-wright, William Shakespeare, and the famous actors who performed his works.

"Now," he said. "Do you know any Shakespeare such as The Tempest, Hamlet and others?"

There was an instant reply from a lady at the back: "I loses mi tempest wi' mi 'usband an' I plays hamlet when he wain't wesh up."

YORKSHIRE SAYING: It's no good retirin', tha nivver gits a day off.

A SNOOTY woman from a town was on holiday in Wharfedale when she glared at an old angler.

"Haven't you anything better to do than catch those poor little fish?" she asked.

"Nay, there's nowt I can do abhat it," he replied. "If this little beggar had kept its mouth shut he'd nowt to fear from me."

He paused for a while and then grinned: "An' the same goes for thee, missus."

An old lady of more than ninety in Bradford was being passed by a hearse, and the road was so narrow that she was almost knocked over. "Ey up," she shouted to the driver, "thee stop bein' greedy."

AN ANGLER was holding a rod into a stream only one foot wide. "Why ister fishin' 'ere?" he was asked.

"Mind thi own business," was the reply. "I'm nobbut showin' t' wife that I's gitten nah time ter peel t' spuds."

AN OLD bachelor was invited to a golden wedding party. He was not sure what all the fuss was about and a relative tried to explain.

"Well, tha sees this man an' woman have lived together for fifty years."

The old lad looked on in disgust. "Well it's reet that he shud mek an honest woman on her at long last."

AN OLD daleswoman had been married four times and her relatives asked her which husband she would have when she went to Heaven.

"Nobbut yan cos I've gitten no choice," she said. "I nivver had t' first three lang enough to reform 'em."

Young Fred

Ah've gorra sister, Milly Ann,
She says us lads is rough
She nivver feights; she laiks wi dolls
An' talks some soppy stuff.

She's flaid o' mice, an' flaid o' bulls
She'll nivver swim in t' beck
An' when ah brings me ferret hoam
She screams like flipping heck.

Ah doen't like lasses much Ah think
it's appen cos they're soft
They don't git muckied up like us
At least not quite as oft.

But mind yer Milly Ann's all reight.
Me muther lets her bake.
Soa we've a secret – me an' 'er
She meks an extra cake.

Will Clemence
YORKSHIRE SAYING: If tha' ivver gets the urge to exercise just thee lie dahn and it'll pass off.

HEARD at a point-to-point meeting: "Yon 'orse is too polite. Afore he cums to a fence he allus stops and lets t' rider gah first."

A TEACHER in a Dales school conducted a general knowledge test. She put a two-shilling piece on the desk and asked, "What is this?"

A small lad at the front took a close look and said, "Heads."

An old dalesman looked closely at a group of ramblers passing through his village. He jerked his thumb at his mate and said, "Them's a reet group of predestin- arians."

A VERY prosperous looking farmer was attending a dinner in Thirsk. He confided to the waitress that he was nearly eighty.

The waitress spilled a little soup on his trousers and apologised, but saying they would not stain so badly.

"Aye 'appen not. These breeches are of good stuff. They belonged to mi father."

A SCHOOL class was asked, "Where did Nicholas Nickleby teach at school?"

"At Dootheboys Hall near Greta Garbo," was one instant reply.

TWO YOUNG lads from Addingham said to the bus conductor, "Three-pence-hawpenny come back."

"What?"

"Three-pence-hawpenny come back," the lad repeated.

The conductor turned to the other lad and asked, "I suppose you want the same?"

"Noa. I wants a two-penny stop theer," was the reply.

THERE WAS an old lady in Thirsk who at ninety-six still ruled her unmarried daughter aged seventy-three with a rod of iron.

"Ee Mary," said the vicar . "You've got a grand daughter there."

"Aye so I 'as," was the reply. "I don't knaw what I'll do when the Lord sees fit to tek 'er away."

A dales farmer decided to get married in his own back yard. He did so that his chickens could eat the rice which was thrown.

OVERHEARD at a Women's Institute lecture: "Tonight I will show you how to kill chickens. Then tomorrow you will be able to kill yourselves."

A YOUNG farm worker from Wharfedale, not noted for his power of speech, was 'keeping company' with a very pretty girl. She was becoming rather tired of his lack of conversation. One evening he had said nothing for nearly half-an-hour when he suddenly said, "Tha's walked aht wi' worse chaps nor me hasn't tha?"

There was no reply and so he repeated the question. "Hod on a bit," she said. "I'm nobbut thinkin'."

An old lady made a daily visit to the churchyard and was asked why she did this. The reply was, "Tha can't believe what a grand feelin' it is to be able to walk aht agin when I's more than ninety!"

A DALES farmer had gone to help a neighbour. Before he went home he sat down in the kitchen to smoke his pipe. He struck a match, lit his pipe and tossed the spent match into the hearth. After all, Captain Webb's matches were a dozen boxes for a penny in those days, so there was no need to keep it.

The farmer's wife thought otherwise. "Ah doan't like to see owt wasted," she said and picked up the spent match with the tongs, held it to the fire and used it to light her candle.

Lament

The're bahn ter mak me goa ter wark.
Me schoolin' days ar' ower
Noa laikin' nah; there'll be noa sun
Ah shan't be hoam at fower.

Noa mour Ah'll call at Saxon's farm
Ter sit wi' pride o' t' mower
Ah'll still be stuck in t' spinnin' mill
– Ah shan't be hoam at fower

Ah'd like ter bin a farmer-lad
But towage's much lower
The're makkin me a pieceneer nah.
– Ah shan't be hoam at fower.

Ah'd reyster walked wi' Saxon's hoss
Ah cud "Gee-up" an' "whoa" 'er
Ah can't thoil t' time for iron mules
– Ah shan't be hoam at fower.

An' when Ah see 'at dayleet' s goan
Ah'll knaw at reapin's ower
How ivver much Ah think on it
– Ah shan't be home at fower."

Will Clemence

TWO DALES farmers met at a local auction mart and discussed electricity and the farms.

"Ah 'ears tha's bin 'avin' it fixed in thi farm. Ah 'opes that tha'll be suited wi' it."

"Aye, it'll be o'reet speshially in t' winter. Any roads, tha can cum up an' see it when t' job's done."

Later his friend called in and was asked how he liked the new lights. "It's o' reet. I can read paper."

"But it's leet nah, why aster gitten leets on?"

"Yan chap wot put 'em in, put 'em in bottles an' Ah can neether blow 'em aht or turn 'em dahn."

KATE WAS a pupil in a dales school and was asked by her teacher for a definition of a Quaker.

"A Quaker is a fella wot nivver gambles, nivver wants to feight an' nivver answers back. Mi dad's a Quaker but mi mother in't."

> *A miserly fella fra Dent*
> *Run off 'stead of payin' his rent.*
> *Cried t' landlord – reight mad –*
> *I'll chase thee mi lad*
> *An 'e did – 'alf oop Penyghent.*

A COOK, having decided to get married, gave notice to her mistress. "What could a man see in you to want to marry you?" was the snobby response.

The cook replied: "There's trimmin' for all sorts o' cloth or else t' master would never have wed thee."

AN OLD dalesman was knocked down by a car driven by a posh lady. He was not badly hurt and when he rose to his feet the woman motorist scolded him for his carelessness.

"It was your fault entirely," she said, "I've been driving a car for ten years and I am very experienced."

"Look thee 'ere missis," said the dalesman, "I's no beginner either. Ah've bin walkin' on these two legs for t' last sixty years!"

Dales Alphabet

A stands for Aysgarth (remember the Falls)

"You're sacked!"
"You what? Can't hear you."
"I said you're sacked."
"Tha'll have to speak up, still can't hear you."
"Oh nivver mind. Ah'll sack someone else."

B is for Beckermonds, with low limestone walls
C gives Cam Houses and Clapham and Cray
D is for Deepdale up Langstrothdale Way
E is East Witton in Yoredale of course
F is for Fossdale Beck (see Hardraw Force)
G gives us Grinton in the one dale we love
H is for Hardraw (see F above)
I's Ingleborough – a magical name
J's Jervaux Abbey of pre-Tudor fame
K is for Kilnsey and Kisden as well
L are the lead mines on Starbotton Fell
M is for Mallerstang (for cycling slow)
N gives us Nethergill (see O below)
O is for Oughtershaw, at beloved Wharfe's tail
P stands for Pateley in dear Nidderdale
Q is a Queer letter so read on beneath
R is for Richmond and Ripon and Reeth
S is for Shunner and the start of the Swale
T is Tan Hill in Arkengarthdale
U is the urge for a fell-climbing hop
V is for victory when we get to the top
W is for Whernside – hill to inspire
X Hollow Mill Cross (see M a bit higher)
Y is for Yockenthwaite (in Langstroth please learn)
Z is my zenith of joy on return

AT A FARM tucked away in a dale, not a thousand miles from Skipton, the farmer's wife was baking, and her bread would not brown. She raked the fire, piled on more fuel, pulled the damper in and out, but, do what she would, the oven refused to 'draw'.

Just as her patience was about exhausted, her husband came for his 'forenoon drinking'. No sooner had he entered the door, and before he could speak, he was faced with a tray full of consumptive looking bread, and his angry wife.

"Si tha," she said. "Tha'll ha' to do summat about that oven. This bread's bin in ower hawf-an-'our, and it's as white as a cap."

The good man shook up his cushion, sat down and quietly replied: "Es ta tried cleaning thi oven out?"

"Hm," she snapped, banging the trayful of cakes on the table. "Tha knows weel enough I allus clean it out, ivvery week, afore I start baking."

"Ay," he answered deliberately, "Ah know tha sticks a brush up t' flue. But, tha knows, av telled tha mony a time, 'a wipe down isn't a wesh'."

OLD MRS Moore was a pattern in contentment. When somebody suggested that her old age pension was a meagre sum, she replied, "Ee, I wouldna like the Lord ti think me unsatisfied – and me with a sack o' pertaters oot i' t' byre."

Two old Bradford weavers were talking

about space travel and one asked, "'As thee ivver sin a flyin' saucer?"

"Nay they don't exist."

"Aye thi do. My wife'll show thi one cos I's late comin' yam agin and she nivver misses."

There's nowt as clean and 'omely
As t' good owd Holmfirth twang.

There's some 'at try their fancy talk
Wi' dialect mixed among
They'd sahnd a lot better
If they'd stick t' Holmfirth twang.

Owd customs are forgotten
Laiking Neets and Riding t' Stang
But owd speiks'll live for ivver
In t' good owd Holmfirth twang.

Be prahd on it, speik it
An' sing it. Guy's hang!
There's nowt to be ashamed on
In t' good owd Holmfirth twang.

GRAND, indomitable, independent, and individual are

the dalesfolk. One reads in foolish London publications that outstanding characters are things of the past, and that humanity has become uniform.

To look at the monotonous appearance of townspeople would seem to bear that out, but in the dales they are just as individual as ever.

On acquiring a Wensleydale cottage, one couple arrived there on a Tuesday, in a wet August. Forgetting that Wednesday would be early closing day, after a busy morning they went down to Hawes to buy food.

All the shops were shut except the greengrocer's. And he might sell only what was perishable. The couple asked for cheese. The grocer replied that he could let them have carrots. They pointed out that carrots were no more perishable than cheese.

"Ah knoa yon," said the old dalesman, witheringly. "But t' law says they is, so of coorse they is."

His wife was in the shop, and seeing the quandary, said to her husband, "Ye might sell 'em a lile bit o' cheese."

The old man, with a cheery smile, went to the door of his shop, looked up and down the street, and said, "Nay, nay, if I sell her a bit I'll see as she has a pretty middlin' big piece."

A SCOT and a Yorkshireman were talking in a railway carriage. The man from the Tweed talked loud and long about what his country could do. The Tyke eventually retaliated: "Tha's bin opening thi mouth for long enough but can thee tell me summat that thi can't do an I'll do it for thi."

"Weel," replied Jock, "Ah canna pay ma fare."

The Lay of the Hiker

'Twas autumn at a Yorkshire inn
The rain pound down without
He entered soaking to the skin –
A hiker and a waterspout.

He'd trodden o'er the sodden moor
He oozed from boot to tie
And as the streams flowed on the floor
"A drink," he cried, "I'm dry!"

A DALES village band arrived home late after winning a band concert. Making sure they did not cause a nuisance they took off their shoes and walked in stocking feet. Then they struck up 'See the Conquering Hero Comes' at full blast and really did disturb the peace.

A FARMER had employed a rather timid young lad and when they were moving part of an old barn a rat ran out and went up the leg of his trousers. The lad was terrified and shouted, "Mr Jinks, sir, wot shall I do?"

"Thee wait theer a bit, lad," said the farmer with a grin. "I'll just go yam an fetch mi gun."

Lullaby for a potholer's baby:

Sleep little stalag-mite
Mother holds her stala-tight
Father's off with torch and rope
Leaving mum with you to cope
Whilst he through limestone caves will forge
'Tis this which sticks in Mother's gorge."

WHEN attending an examination at the medical school in Leeds a student was asked, "Now then young man, what is an Achilles tendon?"

"God knows."

"What is an embolism?"

"God knows," was the confused reply.

He later received a written reply which read: God passed – you failed.

A vicar in Nidderdale told his congregation one Sunday that every blade of grass could be used to inspire a sermon. The next day he was mowing his lawn when one of his flock passed by and called out, "That's reet, vicar, tha should cut thi sermons short."

TWO MEN were sitting in a busy café in Settle. One was

huge and the other was tiny. The little man plucked up courage and asked, "Do you think you could pass me the sugar?"

"Aye lad," was the reply. "I reckon I can manage that all reet. I've bin movin' pianers all mi life."

A DALES farmer and his wife never missed the local Christmas concert but one year the wife had a cold and the old chap went on his own. The choir was always in evidence but so was the local tenor who hit most notes but not the high ones. When he got home the old lady asked how he had enjoyed the concert.

"It was all reet. T' choir sanged t' Hallelujah Chorus and old Bert sang Trumpet Shall Sound."

"Aye, I's not surprised. Wee Bert Danson 'e allus tried to be different to t'others."

A LAD from Leyburn had to go to London on the train. Light refreshments were sold on the journey. The waiter approached and asked, "Would you like two poached eggs on toast sir?"

"Aye – I suppose so. It'll be reet to me if tha's not gitten any plates."

A YOUNG girl from near Skipton returned from a visit to the dentist. Her mother asked, "Did 'e 'urt thi lass?"

"Nah, nut a lot but he didn't 'alf yell when I bit 'is finger," said the girl.

THIS IS not about the first Chinese take-away in Leyburn but was overheard in a draper's shop; "Dun yer wishens weshen well?" Which, when translated, means – "Do your new cushions wash well?"

Taken from an essay written by a pupil from the dales: "There are three kinds of clergymen – bishops, vikers and curats. The bishop tells the vikers to work and the curats do it. A curat is usually a thin man but when he is a viker he gets fatter and preaches longer sermons and becomes a good man."

A TRAIN stopped at Skipton station and was only wait-

ing for a few minutes. A passenger poked his head out and spoke to a small boy who was train spotting.

"Hey, sonny," he shouted, "Go an' get me a pork pie and get one for thiself."

Just as the train was setting off the breathless lad with his mouth full of pie shouted, "There were nobbut one left."

TEACHER to a little lass: "What does BC mean?"
    "Before Christ."
    "What does AD mean?"
    "After the devil."

A FARMER in the dales approached the vicar asking him to pray for rain.
    "No I'm afraid I cannot do that."
    "What?" said the farmer. "Why not?"
    "Because," said the vicar, "there's a hole in the vicarage roof."

AN OLD farmer was glaring at his grand-daughter who had dug up and was peeling potatoes: "Ee lass. Thi sent that much muck on these tatties that I'll 'ev no farm left in a bit."

AN ELDERLY lady in Pontefract was ill but was reluctant to go to see the doctor. When asked why, she said, "I don't want to upset 'im. He gets upset when any on us is badly."

DURING the First World War a lad from Leeds was in a

line where a burly sergeant was taking down soldiers' particulars.

"Religion?" he growled.

"Eh?" replied the recruit.

"What are you man, Baptist, Church of England, Methodist or what?"

"Prudential," was the reply.

A MAN who had been married three times tied the knot for the fourth time. His new wife found three hats in a drawer wrapped up in tissue paper.

"Wot's them for?" she asked.

"They're from t' other three wives. I thowt I'd keep 'em."

"Well," was the reply, "they be going into t' fire and t' next un to be kept in yon drawer will be thy cap."

There was an old dalesman who had electricity installed in his house. Sometime later the man called to read the meter. He was surprised how little had been used. When asked, the lady of the house said, "We nobbut put a leet on so as to find our way to t' paraffin lamp."

IN THE Second World war an old lady from Hawes was

asked to buy some war bonds. "Nay," she said, "I don't believe in none o' them banks. I keeps all mi brass in mi own tin box."

"But," was the reply, "you have forgotten about the interest."

"Nay I 'evn't. I put in a bit extra each week to cover that."

OVERHEARD in a Gargrave pub where two anglers were discussing their catch. One said, "My pike were so big that when I landed it t' canal watter went down a foot."

"That's nowt," said the other. "Last week I copped yan so big that it had to git out to let canal boats pass."

ON A LOVELY summer's morning in the dales during the war an old lad was watching haymaking in full swing. He stood watching the Land Girls who were employed on the farm. At last he could contain himself no longer. He leaned over the wall and said, "It's cum ti summat when we've putten lasses in t' pants."

AN EVANGELIST was ranting on in the market place at Thirsk and he shouted, "I's led a good life but I'se worried how I'll git mi wings ower mi shirt when I dees."

A voice from the crowd shouted, "Don't thee worry, lad. Tha'll nivver get the trousers o'er thi tail."

THE OLD pump which stands near the market cross in

Askrigg has not been in use for years but when it had a utilitarian as well as a decorative value it was responsible for evoking one of those pithy remarks at which dalesmen can be so adept.

One of the older residents of the village recalls that some forty years ago the pump became clogged and would not work properly. The village blacksmith of the period, who professed to a wide knowledge of any type of machinery, undertook to put the pump in order.

After the expert had filled the market place with tools and spent the best part of a day on the task, the pump still refused to work; in fact, it was worse. Then a villager called Ben stepped quietly in and righted the wrong in a very short space of time and without any fuss.

When the pump was functioning again, Ben, who ever after was dubbed 'Pump Ben', was asked, "What did thou use to clean t' pump out, Ben, some special tool?"

"No," replied Ben, "nobbut superior knowledge."

A MAN taking a walk around some allotments stopped by a fine crop of potatoes.

"What brand are those?" he asked.

"Great Scott," replied the gardener.

The man, knowing little about potatoes, but not to be outdone by what he thought was a sarcastic reply, said, "I've got a decent crop too."

"And what brand are yours?" asked the rustic.

"Good Heavens," was the reply.

Harry stood at the Pearly Gates

His face was worn and old.
He meekly asked the man of fate
Admission to the fold.
What have you done St Peter said
To seek admission here?
I kept a Guiseley fish shop
For many and many a year.
The gate flew open widely
As Peter pressed the bell
Come in old man and take a harp
Tha's 'ad enough of hell.

ON A BOILING hot day a holidaymaker at Filey was making sand sculptures for his children and produced a very life-like model of a baby elephant. He took off his cap, mopped his brow and put the cap on the elephant's back. He then fell asleep, only to be awoken by his children who were watching passers-by throwing coins into his cap.

A farmer asked his ploughman why he wanted to be paid monthly instead of weekly. The man replied, "Well, me an' t' wife allus 'as a row ivvery pay day."

A LOCAL lad was batting for the village cricket team

and kept swiping at the ball but hitting nothing. Two old lads were watching the game when one said to the other, "Ee's no good is 'ee?"

"Nah, but I've gitten a job for 'im."

"A job?"

"Aye, I need a gardener and 'ee'll be reet for swiping dahn mi nettles."

ON THE Grassington bus operated by the West Yorkshire Road Company the driver thought he had run over a goose. The conductor looked through the rear window and saw a cloud of white feathers. When they arrived back at the depot the goose was found and removed from the back axle, black as the fire-back and almost devoid of feathers. The following day they returned the goose to a farmer who said, "Tha's a grand lad; but it's nobbut half roasted."

A CHEMIST was just about to close when a young lad ran in and said, "I wants me mother to stink an' she's sent thee a note."

The confused chemist looked at it and finally understood. The note read, OH DICK ALONE IN A SMALL BOCKLE.

A WENSLEYDALE grocer was busy and looking harassed. "I's sorry tha'll 'ev to carry thee own shopping Jessie," he said to a very old lady. "Mi reet-'and-man's off ill wi' a swollen foot."

THE LOCAL brass band in a dales village was not noted

for 'in-tune' performances. The conductor was asked, "Wot's t' next piece we's playin'?"

"Handel Largo," was the reply.

The trombone player looked at his music sheets and said, "Aw gawd, I just played that."

A PREACHER was on his way to a service when he was given a lift by a farmer in his horse and trap. Suddenly the animal bolted, and the scared preacher said, "I would give five pounds to be out of this."

The farmer responded, "Thee stick wi' thi brass lad, tha'll be aht for nowt in a minute."

A DOCTOR told of a young couple who lived in a

"Ah've telled ye afore abaht standin' gossipin' i' this kind o' weather."

remote farm in the dales who were worried about their young baby. The doctor stayed with the family until the little one improved.

"He'll be fine once he's had a good sleep," said the doctor and made his weary way home. The doctor himself was sound asleep when he was awoken by a shower of pebbles striking his bedroom window. He looked out to see the young father waving to him from the garden.

"It's a' reet, doctor. I've just run dahn to tell thi that baby's sleepin' reet peaceful nah."

A RIPON resident had just been fitted with a brand new set of dentures. A few days later a friend visited the old lady who was hard at work cleaning but not wearing her new teeth. After a few minutes the friend asked, "Is ter nut wearin' thi' new teeth. Is they 'urtin thi?"

"Nah, these is a' reet but I's nut paying fourteen-pahnd-ten for teeth just to clean up in."

A DALES doctor spoke to a patient: "Do you know you've been walking about with a bone broken in your back? Why haven't you come to me before?"

"Well lad," said the old farmer, "Ivvery time I sez summat's wrang wi' me t' wife tells me to stop smokin'."

A FIRM of dales builders had to go to a remote farm to do some work. They sent an apprentice to hire a horse.

"How long will you want it?" asked the farmer.

"We want t' longest tha's got. There's five on us."

An old Yorkshire farmer was visited in his isolated farm by an eager young relative. He looked at the old man's decrepit radio set and suggested that he should buy a new one. "Nah lad, I'm ower old for a change. An' any roads I've nobbut just got used to fowk in t' old un."

A TOURIST passing through Barnsley asked where the nearest lake was.

"Reet 'ere," was the reply.

"Where?" asked the puzzled tourist.

"It's 'ere. I allus laiks on a Monday an' if mi 'orse wins on Sat'day I laiks all week."

A WOMAN took her husband to a doctor's surgery for a check-up. The woman never stopped talking long enough for the doctor to get on with his job. He slipped a thermometer in her mouth and told her to stick it under her tongue. He then got on with treating the old dalesman who grinned at the doctor. "How much does yan on them things cost?" he asked with a sly wink.

TWO YORKSHIRE builders were discussing the day's news and one of them said: "I read summat in t' paper this mornin' wot I don't fathom. It said an airman had to bale out. I didn't knaw they carried watter with 'em."

TWO ELDERLY daleswomen met up in the post office.

"How's old Maud keepin'?"

"She's none so good."

"Wot's up?"

"She's gitten chronic constipation. She's down t' closet for hours."

"Has she taken owt?"

"Oh aye, she taken to takin' 'er knittin'."

AT A MARKET in Batley two old lads were having a good natter.

"Whear's ta bin?"

"Ah's bin gittin wed. Ah thowt I'd like somebody to close mi eyes when Ah's dead."

"Well Ah've bin wed twice and both of 'em hev opened mine."

JONT went a-courting the Dent schoolmistress. Each evening as she sat knitting, Jont pulled out her needles, letting her stitches drop.

Always, without reproach but with seemingly unending patience, Mary picked up the stitches and knitted it up again. This continued week after week. Jont boasted to his pals that he'd "gitten t' best-tempered woman in t' world."

The wedding day dawned. As they walked home over the bridge after the ceremony, Mary turned to Jont, her eyes ablaze – but not with love – and snarled, "Now Ah'll ravel thee."

A FARM LAD was carrying home the last load of hay from field to barn and an irate motorist behind him was trying to pass. As the lad turned towards the barn the motorist shouted at him, "Why didn't you pull over and let me pass? You must have heard me hooting."

"Aye, I heard thi a' reet but 'ow did I knaw tha were in a hurry when tha was nobbut goin' t' same speed as me?"

IN THE DAYS when cameras were not so sophisticated as they are today, a keen photographer not noted for his generosity went on holiday to Whitby. There he saw and photographed a poor old lady looking hungry. He asked if he could take her photograph and she told him that she'd had nothing to eat for two days and was cold.

"What did you give her?" asked a more generous friend.

"Well as it were rainin' I gave her 1/100th of a second at f8," was the reply.

A hardworking young housewife from Leeds was being discussed.

"Ee Jack, tha's gitten a reet grand lass theer."

"Aye," was the reply "She nivver stops working. I wish I'd gitten two more like 'er."

AN ABSENT-minded bishop on his way to a meeting could not find his ticket when the collector arrived in his carriage. After a long search the collector said, "It's alreet reverend. I'll trust thee. Don't bother looking for it."

"I'll have to find it," said the worried bishop, "I need to know where I'm going."

> *Me father deed when I wor young,*
> *An' left ma all his riches,*
> *A feather bed, a wooden leg,*
> *An' a pair o' leather britches,*
> *A coffee pot wi'art a spart,*
> *A teea kettle wi'art a hannel,*
> *A 'bacca box wi'art a snap,*
> *An' hauf a fard'd cannel.*

AN AMBITIOUS young couple bought a pub called the Stags Head. They did not like hunting and asked the not-too-pleased locals to come up with the new name. One said, "Worra baht, Walk Inn an' Stagger Aht?"

A DALESMAN'S definition of an owl – a grand rat-catcher wot costs nowt to feed.

A FARMER'S wife was commenting on a new hand who was not very tidy. She looked briefly into the lad's bed-room and growled to her husband, "Ah doan't knaw wither to bed him dahn or muck 'im aht."

A SMALL village lad had very big feet, and his father said to a friend, "Ee'd a bin a reet tall un if 'ee 'adn't ower much turned up at t' bottom."

Getting up in the morning is just a case of mind over mattress.

A WIDOWER who 'enjoyed' bad health surprised his friends when he suddenly got married one November to a lady much older than himself. When asked why he chose this lady he replied, "Nah doant thee worry. She's reet good at choppin' wood and she's a reet good cook. I's sure she'll last me all ower t' winter."

A BOY writing home to his parents from his public school wrote: "I was in a performance called Hamlet. Although some people had seen it before, they laughed just the same."

A YOUNG girl was asked what a map was. She replied, "It's a bit o' paper wot 'elps thee git lost."

A DALES farmer was getting fed up with an Agricultural Inspector. He was filling in form after form and wanted to get back to his farm workers. Then his pen ran out of ink and the inspector, himself not too pleased, said, "Come on, man, put your weight on it."

The farmer glared at him and said, "Fowerteen-stone-ten-pahnds, lad. What's thine?"

THERE IS a story of a Skipton lady who was travelling on a bus to Harrogate. To pass the time she began to count the number of times she heard the word 'Aye' on the crowded bus and thought about her view that Yorkshire men did not waste words.

"Bad weather int it?"

"Aye."

"Did you get your harvest in?"

"Aye."

"Christmas will soon be with us."

Aye."

The lady counted 103 'ayes' before she went to sleep to be woken up as the conductor shouted, "This is 'Arrogate."

"Aye," said the lady and got off.

IN A VILLAGE on the outskirts of Sheffield an election meeting was held at which the candidate was to speak. As he was addressing other meetings the same evening and transport was by horse-drawn vehicle, there could be no exact timing for the meeting to start.

To keep the audience in good humour during the period of waiting, one stalwart led community singing. Having gone through their repertoire of popular songs, they turned to hymns.

After continued delay someone struck up, "Hold the fort for I am coming."

As they sang, "See the mighty host advancing, Satan leading on," the candidate walked on to the platform followed by ardent supporters.

MRS A CALLED on her friend Mrs C. After a little conversation, Mrs C suddenly broke off, took a pint pot from the side of the kitchen sink, half filled it with water, and rushed to the back door, where she discharged its contents on a young cockerel which had just crowed. Then she returned and said, "I allus keeps that pot 'andy for that daft bird."

Mrs A replied, "Why, what's wrong with a cock crowing? It's the nature of the bird."

"Aye," said Mrs C, "that may be soa, but yer see we're not allowed to keep fowls in these 'ere council 'ouses, an' ya nivver know who might be walkin' around. Ah'll cure it yet."

When asked by her teacher to describe a lake, the little lass from the dales replied, "It's a girt bit o' watter wi land all rahnd it."

THE VILLAGE joiner was annoyed with the new lad, the result of whose first day's work was a huge pile of shavings and a rickety-looking milking stool.

"Well," said the boss, "I've been in t' trade sixty years and I've never seen a worse looking stool."

"Nay," said the lad, "tha's got a shock coming when tha shifts yon heap o' shavings."

FOUR farmers went to the field by a haunted quarry at dusk to try to catch a dog that was worrying sheep. Peter and Bob were together. Bob was waiting for Peter, who suddenly came running to him, shaking with fear.

"I've seen a man wi'out an' 'ead," he gasped.

Bob replied: "Doan't worry, Peter. If he's gotten no head, he can't see thee."

A philosopher is a chap who doesn't want what he can't get.

AT A FARM not many miles from Sedbergh a walker was very kindly invited by the farmer's wife to stay for tea. While the meal was being prepared, the farmer and visitor talked on a number of local topics, and the vicar of that particular parish was mentioned. His powers as a preacher were summed up by the farmer, who said: "By gum 'e's clever; 'e can preach sich a sermon as ther' isn't a skulemaister i' aw Sedber' can understand!"

TROUBLE is like a cat's back. There are two ways to stroke it.

A DALESWOMAN, looking very harassed on her doorstep, was asked by a tourist how many children she had. She thought for a bit and said, "Well nah, I's gitten one 'ere on mi lap, one crawler, one in t' pram in t' back yard and a young un runnin' abaht in t' garden. If tha cums back next year there'll be another un."

A cowman in Wensleydale was asked how he started his day: "I turn aht t' hoil lamp in mi cottage and then switch on t' electric leet in t' cowshed."

A TIMID motorist in North Yorkshire stopped his car and asked an elderly lady at her garden gate if the road hereabouts is dangerous.

"Nut 'ere it int; it's down theer at bottom where they all kills thisells."

In Praise of a Monk

Nah why 'ee's so plump the reason I'll tell;
'Im as lives a good life is bahn to live well.
What baron or squire
Or yon knight of the shire
Lives so well as yon holy frier?

A YOUNG lady from Leeds was boasting to her grandfather who lived in Dales. "I've got my own personal trainer and go to the gym," she said.

"My personal trainer costs nowt," said the old man, "He's called Rover and has four legs and a tail."

A Visit to a Shipley Cinema

Ah went to the Palace tomorrow
An' took a front seat at the back
I bowt a plain teacake wi' raisins in
An' buttered it ower wi' fat.

A VERY wealthy and bombastic Bradford wool merchant went for a drive in the dales along a narrow road which overlooked a steep valley. He met a very old car, and neither driver would give way.

He said to the other driver, "What's the car worth?"

When he was told, he paid the man three times what it was worth and pushed it over the edge.

A DALESMAN met a townie who was on a walking tour: "Why ister walking sa fast?"

"I do twenty miles a day, old man, and I walk on my toes."

The old man smiled and said, "Has ter gitten blisters on thi 'eels?"

DENT HAS always been famous for the longevity of its natives. A traveller saw a seventy-year-old man crying on his doorstep and asked what the matter was. "My fadder's just given me a cloutin' fer throwin' stones at mi granddad," was the reply.

A four year old looked at a young baby in its pram. The boy infant was red in the face and crying. "I know wot's up wi him. He's cryin' cos when he went aht he forgot to put his false teeth in."

A DALES FARMER had a disagreement with his land-lord and finally decided to take his case to court. Discussing the possibilities of winning it he asked his barrister, "'Ow would it be if I sent t' owd judge a couple o'ducks?"

"If you want to lose your case that's the way to do it," was the stern reply.

After coming out of court having won his case the farmer turned to his barrister and said, "Ah sent t' ducks to t' judge."

"Surely you didn't?" asked the worried barrister.

"Aye, I sent 'em in t' landlord's name," was the reply accompanied by a broad wink.

THE FOREMAN of a jury was illegally approached by a friend of a man accused of murder and was offered £20 to persuade the twelve men of true to bring in a verdict of manslaughter. In due course this verdict was upheld and the man only got one year in prison. The man handed over the £20 and said, "I never expected him to get away so lightly. How did you manage it?"

The foreman looked at the jury members who were all battered and bruised. "It weren't easy," he grinned, "ten on 'em wanted to acquit 'im."

A BOAT was leaving Hull for Rotterdam. A steward was explaining the boarding and shouted, "First class forward, second class aft."

He looked at a very young lass carrying a baby in her arms. He asked, "First or second, madam?"

"Don't thee be so daft. It's not mine, it's mi mother's."

A DALESMAN won a large prize in a raffle but he still looked glum. "Wot's the matter wi thee?" a friend asked.

"Aye, one ticket were all reet, but I got two an' I've wasted t' other."

IN THE GOOD old days an old daleswoman had spent nearly an hour trying to get a phone call through in the kiosk. A huge queue built up around her. Eventually the old lass was escorted out by a post office official who had been called. She came out reluctantly and protesting that it wouldn't work. It wasdiscovered that she had picked up the receiver and then hung her umbrella on the hook.

A YOUNG lad was proud of his dog and a stranger asked him, "What sort of a dog is it?"

"It's a black lavatory door," he said.

The labrador did not look insulted but just wagged his tail.

AN ELDERLY lady for once travelled on an early bus into Bingley on a spring morning. She was greeted by an old gentleman who had not seen her for some time. He said, "Ey up Alice. I's nut sin thee fer a bit. Has tha bin inebriatin' for t' winter?"

A Gardener's Lament

At t' low side o' my Uncle Ben's orchard
'E grows farish o' taties and fruits;
But 'owever much rain t' Lord sends 'im
Seems it nivver gits dahn inter t' roots.

Well this mornin' 'is orchard were flooded
Rahnd 'is taties swam t' moor'ens an' coots.
For a wonder me uncle wor laughin'
"By gawd lads, it's got dahn into t' roots".

J Winterburn

A DALESMAN had all his teeth out and asked why he had done this he replied, "It's t' only way I could stop misel bitin' mi nails."

ENTRY on a Yorkshire gravestone:

> *"Here lies a woman,*
> *No men can deny it;*
> *She died in peace, although she lived unquiet.*
> *Her husband prays, if e'er this way you walk,*
> *You would tread softly – if she wakes she'll talk."*

AN OLD lady from a remote dale, looking at television for the first time, saw a golf tournament. She looked at it for a long while and then said, "Ee – they'd knock on a lot wicker if them bumps were flattened a' they filled up all o' them 'oles."

A LITTLE lass loved feeding the ducks by the mill dam at Tickhill. There was a birthday party and the vicar was one of the guests. He saw that the little girl was bored and suggested that she went for a walk.

"Aye, I will."

"Where will you go?" asked the vicar.

"I's off to feed the dam ducks," said the lass to the very confused vicar.

A SIGNWRITER had two adverts in his shop window. One read: "I made signs afore I could talk"

And the other was a brief poem:

> *"We have distemper*
> *it's not infectious*
> *You can buy it in tins."*

"Actually, you'll be learning on something smaller."

AN AMERICAN visitor to Harrogate was explaining to a man on a train the shortcomings of rail travel in Yorkshire. He said, "In my country you can ride all day in a train and never leave the state we live in."

The Yorkshireman replied, "Ee, that's reet bad for thee. Our trains nivver run that slow."

TWO YOUNG men went out shooting rabbits but they were both very poor shots.

"Dosta think we should gah yam?" asked one.

"Nah. We'll miss two o' three moo-er and then we'll gah yam."

A FARMER was getting fed up with his wife moaning at him. One day she said, "Tha's still nut been reet sensible. I've a good mind to leave thi altigither."

"Reet then," was the reply. "Let me knaw wheer tha's goin' an' I'll cum wi' thi."

A DALES farmer was visited by the vicar who was about to christen the family's first son and asked for the name.

"We're callin 'im Homer."

"I did not know you were a classical scholar and knew all about the old poet?" the vicar replied.

"Nah reverend – I keeps pigeons."

A FARMER employed two new lads to work as ploughmen. "To git a straight furrow tha finds summat to fix thi eye on and tha follers that."

Two hours later one lad had ploughed a straight furrow but the other lad's furrow was twisted.

"What line did tha foller?" asked the farmer.

"Well boss, I watched yon white cow and it were goin' all ower t' place."

An old mill worker in Keighley never married and was known for his meanness. He was taken ill and one of his neighbours said, "If 'ee dees he'll cum on to me to lend him a coffin."

A YOUNG lady teacher of ample girth was trying hard to keep her class interested.

"Now children," she said, "let us talk about the letter H. This stands for hippopotamus. Anyone who wants to know what a hippopotamus looks like – please look at me."

A MILKMAN near Hawes was suddenly in trouble with three of his neighbours for not presenting them with a bill and the money they had been saving to pay was building up. Suddenly he presented them with a rather large bill.

"Why's tha not bin askin' fer thi brass?" asked one dalesman.

"Well, tha sees, mi dowter's gittin' married next week and I's bin savin up to gi' 'er a reet good send-off."

YORKSHIRE can truly be said to be the birthplace of pantomime. In the 1870s the Grand Theatre in Leeds presented Blue Beard and one set featured a backdrop of Kirkstall Abbey and the then very polluted river Aire. This was shown as blue as the Mediterranean Sea. One wag from the audience shouted out, "Ey up. Yon water's bin filtered."

A SIGN in an old cobbler's shop read:

"Boys and girls well leathered here."

AN OLD car broke down and was towed into a garage near Halifax. "What will it cost to fix it?" asked the owner.

"It'll cost thee quite a lot, an' that's nobbut an estimate," was the reply.

A MAN returning home after a night out and driving under the influence, told a policeman, "Cumin' 'ome I drove into t' wrong drive and ran into a tree wot I have not got."

AN OLD daleswoman was out for a stroll admiring the spring flowers in her local woods. A car drew up with a family of children and began to pick lots of flowers which they piled into the boot. The mother smiled at the old lady and asked, "Can I take this road to Leeds?"

"Aye lass," was the reply, "tha might as weel, tha's taken ivverything else."

Here lies an old woman who always was tired,
She lived in a house where help wasn't hired
Her last words on earth were, "Dear friends I am going
To where there's no washing or charring or sewing.
I'll be where loud anthems will always be ringing,
But having no voice I'll be quit of the singing,
And everything there will be exact to my wishes,
For there they don't eat there'll be no washing of dishes
Don't mourn for me now; don't mourn for me never.
I'm going to do nothing for ever and ever."

Hubert Dumville

A VICAR'S wife in the dales was helping to process a group of evacuees from a slum area of a city. The supervisor was horrified to see that she had written VD against the names of three of the children. When asked to explain she pointed to her shorthand notes which were C meaning clean, D meaning dirty and VD meaning very dirty.

A LAD HAD taken his lass to the pictures but the lass came home in tears.

"Wot's up lass?" asked the anxious mother.

"He nobbut took me in t' sixpenny seats," she wailed.

"Well maybe he's hard up. Tek it back to him."

The lass arrived at the lad's house even though it was late and when he answered her knock she said, "I've browt thi tanner back. Mi mother ses tha needs it more than we do."

"Nay," he replied "tha needn't hev bothered toneet. It wud hev done in t' mornin'."

A WOMENS Institute secretary wrote to a supplier: "Please send to us a new copy of the words of Jerusalem. Our words are very dirty."

A NOT very bright dalesman called Alf kept pigeons. He was taking his racers to the station to be sent off to enter the race.

"Ista sendin' thi pigions off?" he was asked.

"How many ista sendin'?"

"If tha guesses reet thi ken 'ave 'em both," was Alf's response.

"Two!" was the immediate reply.

"That's nut fair," he said, "sumbody's telled thi."

IN THE 1920s there was a popular song sung by Ernie Mayne on a gramophone record. The chorus went:

Chips and fish, chips and fish
Ee by gum, it's a champion dish
Oh what a smell when you fry 'em
Just buy a pennorth try 'em
Put some salt and vinegar on,
As much as ever you wish
You can do without a supper
When you get a pennorth of chips.

A YOUNG boy returned home to tell his father that he was second in his class and the top pupil was a girl.

"Tha can't be beat by a mere girl," said his father.

"You have to realise, dad, that girls aren't as mere as they used to be."

TWO OLD daleswomen were discussing a farmer who had just died but had not been very good to his wife.

"Aye," said one, "he 'edn't bin a good 'usband but she put 'im away aw reet – there was two sorts o' meat in t' funeral tea."

TWO LOCALS were discussing a friend who had lost a lot of weight.

"He's that thin nah," said one, "he's like an 'aporth o' soap after a long day's wesh."

A HALIFAX man was setting off to work and found he was being followed by his two terriers. He shouted back to his wife, "Shoot dogs."

He was instantly attacked by the vicar's wife who told him he was cruel and wicked. The man looked surprised and said, "I nobbut asked me missus to 'shoo' 'em to go back yam."

A VICAR had been transferred from one parish to another. One of his new flock met one of the old flock.

"How does tha like thi new parson?"

"He's a fine chap, a really grand fella but he's a little bit bellicose."

"Nay lad, that's queer, that is. When we 'ad him he were as thin as a lath."

Now do you see why we've always to use a yoke?

A MAN from the dales was staying in a guesthouse on the coast and to say the least the landlady did not serve decent portions.

"Would you fancy an egg for your tea?" she asked.

"Aye lass, and can thi include hen wot laid it?"

Addl'n' Brass

There's monny a way ter addle brass:
An Ah've tried a few missen,
Like 'elpin' aht at haytime
Or muckin' aht a pen.

Ah'm trying nah to addle some.
Ah've spied a fishin' rod,
A reight good greenheart – vary dear
But one yer'd love to hod.

Ah axed all rahnd for wark ter do;
The'd nawther hay ner corn
'Twor then Ah med mi mind up –
Ah'd start ahrt on mi own.

Ah got me wooden barrer aht
An rahnd t' stables took it.
Cos t' chaps dahn at allotments
Ull pay a bob a bucket.

Will Clemence

A YOUNG couple from Leeds were coming home on the train from Scarborough. The husband looked so miserable that his wife asked, "Nah then, Barney, why is tha so sad?"

"Cos we be skint," he moaned.

"No we's not. I put two pahnd in t' tea caddy afore we went."

"Aye," he said, "an' I fahnd it."

DURING the war a farmer was explaining the work to be done to a new Land Army lass fresh from the town. She had to take a horse and cart and bring home a load of turnips.

"Yon hoss," he said, "is a quiet hoss, but tha must make sure that the rein don't touch his back."

At dinner he asked how the lass had done.

"It was fine. There were one or two showers but I kept the rain off him by covering him over with my coat."

When asked for the definition of an earthquake a young lad from the dales replied to his teacher, "It's when Jimmy God starts chuckin' muck abaht."

TWO LADIES who met on a bus had not seen each other for some time. "How's thi bin keeping?" asked one.

"Ah's bin ever so busy. Ah've 'ad all mi teeth aht an' had a new grate put in."

A DALES farmer almost missed the bus on the way to Settle market.

"Ee Josh," said the conductor, "I've never known thee so late."

"Aye, I'd bin waitin' for an 'en to lay an egg so as to make up a dozen."

ONE OLD farmer was always too fond of a drink. He was on his way home with his two horses and a cart when he passed right over a bowling green and fell asleep. Kind villagers released the horses and took them to a stable until he woke up. Next morning he was still hung up and asked a passer-by, "If mi name be Billy Jinks I've lost two 'osses and if I aint Ah's fund a good cart."

Two little sisters were fed up with being sent to church and then to Sunday school. One said to the other, "I wish our mum weren't so devotious."

A SHOOTER with no knowledge of what was 'reet to eat' opened his bag and produced a merganser. He asked the local poacher how to cook the bird. He got both a reply and a smile:

"Put it in a dish wi' a brick. Cover 'em both up with a big slice of bacon fat. Cook him in a hot oven for three hours. Take 'em both out of t' oven. Chuck the bird away and eat the brick."

AN ELDERLY daleswoman was shown a picture of a view of Greta Bridge painted by John Sell Cotman. She looked at some of the houses depicted in the work and then said, "Aye, I bet they 'ev a reet grand view frae yan o' them winders."

> *Sunday school concerts have allus bin held*
> *But there int many on 'em these days*
> *Young folk nivver 'as time to eat*
> *Nivver mind actin' i' concerts and plays.*
>
> *Ah cud go on abaht this for ivver*
> *Of days Ah'll nivver forget*
> *An' when ivver yon is fed up of yon telly*
> *We might cum back to 'em yet.*
> John Roberts (1959)

"DID YON sow have 'er young uns?" asked the youngest of ten children.

"Aye."

"Ow many did she 'eve?"

"Thirteen."

"But she's nobbut got twelve teets. How does t' other manage?"

"It 'as to wait patient, like; like me in our 'ouse."

AN OLD lady was finding it hard to walk and as she struggled back from the privy was heard to say, "I's comin' slow and steady – just like a donkey's gallop."

A VERY pretty young woman ran into a Leeds police station and in floods of tears said, "I want you to find mi 'usband. He's disappeared. Here's is photograph and I want thi to find him."

The young copper looked closely at her photograph and said, "Why?"

OVERHEARD on a Wakefield bus: "Hurry along," shouted the conductress, "use both sides please."

A very large lady replied with a laugh, "Nay lass. I can't do that. I'd 'ev to cut misel i' two."

IN A YORKSHIRE country vicarage there once lived a vicar, his son and his grandson. As was the custom in those days there were three generation of Johns living in the same house. The vicar's wife answered the phone and the person at the other end asked to speak to John: "Which one do you want – John the father, John the son or John the holy terror?"

A BUSY businessman employed a young lass to help with the book-keeping. The day after she started she burst into his office shouting, "Where is it? Where is it?"

Her boss replied "Where's what?"

"I've bin looking all ower t' shop for t' confinement book."

TWO BINGLEY lads were looking at a statue which was labelled 'Sir Titus Salt Bart'. One asked, "What Bart?"

"Cos he's gitten no 'at on," was the reply.

Paintin'

They've painted t' lamp posts into village
it's taken a few days to get dried.
Ah tested 'em all ivvery mornin',
Mi finger marks showed where I tried.

Yon painters got dry 'fore paint did;
They left loads o' bottles by t' wall,
Ah git two pence a piece on them empties,
So mi time weren't wasted at all.

Will Clemence

A LONDONER was holidaying on the Yorkshire coast and spoke to an old lad in his cottage at the top of a cliff. The Londoner said as he looked inside a barn, "These old places can't have much fresh air."

"Thee listen 'ere," was the reply. "Mooer fresh air cums into mi keyole than thou gets in all o' London."

WHEN TRIPS to London by train became possible for dalesfolk the excursion was popular. One old chap and his wife were gazing in wonder at the Mansion House and the traffic when a young policeman being friendly said, "Busy ain't it?"

"Aye," said the dalesman. "There's a trip frae Hawes wot's just come in."

A YOUNG lad from the dales was taken to town and told to go and buy a cap.

"What size?" asked the assistant.

"Ee, I doan't knaw," replied the puzzled lad. "Mi brother teks six-and-seven-eighths an' I's older than 'im so I'll tek nine-and-ten-eighths but it 'as to 'ave a neb on t' top."

TWO LADS were watching Len Hutton scoring lots of runs in a match played at Scarborough. One said, "I've been told that 'utton's eyesight's goin'."

The reply was instant. "Well 'e must 'ev a good sense o' smell."

ONE COLD night a man with reputedly poor eyesight was driving a friend home. The frost was thick on the windows and after a couple of near accidents the friend suggested it might help if he cleaned the windscreen. "Nah, don't thee bother. I's left mi glasses at 'ome."

THE FOLLOWING conversation took place between two farmers owning a similar number of hens.

Fred: "'Ow many eggs dosta git fro' thi 'ens?"

Jack: "Fifty a day on a average."

Fred then went to the shop close to the market. "I's wentin' to buy two Haverages."

"A haverage," asked the confused assistant, "what does it look like?"

"Ah don't knaw but my mate has yan and he gets fifty eggs a day on a Haverage, an' I wants two."

A VICAR began his weekly sermon thus: "My dear friends, you will remember that I promised to speak to you about liars and then I asked you to read the seventeenth chapter of St Mark. How many of you did this?"

A shower of hands went up.

"Thank you," said the vicar. "As there are only sixteen chapters in St Mark my subject today will not be inappropriate."

A North Yorkshire farmer once bought a calf with a long pedigree. A few weeks later a friend asked how the calf was doing. "Oh! Yon calf deed about a fortneet ago, but don't worry, I's still gitten its pedigree."

TWO MARRIED anglers were returning home after a day's fishing when one turned to the other and asked, "Wot's tha 'evin for thi supper toneet."

"Oh it'll be grouse an' tongue as usual," was the reply with a sheepish grin.

A minister always made a point of saying to the pub landlord that he was making money out of beer. One day the publican came across the minister in the street. On taking a pound note out of his pocket he asked if the minister would accept dirty money. "Aye, course I will. The devil's had it long enough."

A FARMER promised his son that if he passed the School Certificate examination he should have a bicycle as a reward. The boy failed and there was the inevitable inquest. "Well tha's lost thi bike. Whatever hest tha bin doin'?" asked the father.

"Trying to learn to ride a bike," was the rueful answer.

IN A SCHOOL in Nidderdale a new teacher asked her class, "Tell me five things found in milk."

One little lass raised her hand and said

"Butter, cheese, ice cream an' twa cows."

A SMALL boy came home from school looking very worried. He told his mother that he was known to the other lads as 'Big Head'.

"Don't thee bother thisel, lad," said the comforting mother, "Ah'm sewer there's nowt in it."

A SCOTTISH visitor to a dales school posed a question and offered sixpence to a child who answered: "Who was the greatest man in history?"

"Robert the Bruce, sir," said an eager lad.

"Well done," said the visitor and gave him the sixpence.

When the visitor had gone the teacher asked the child, "Why did you say that?"

The answer came glibly. "Ah knowed really that it were Len Hutton but business is business."

A COUPLE near Kirkby Lonsdale had only one child. They ran a poultry farm and had an orchard.

Young Jack gazed in wonder at a gander with huge wings. He then thought that at Christmas when some geese were killed he would fasten some wings to his arms and fly. He climbed into an apple tree and tried his luck only to fall with a bump.

His mother rushed out and shouted, "Wot's matter, Jack. Aster fell?"

"I'se been tryin' to fly," he said, rubbing his bruises.

"'Ow did tha manage?" asked his mother.

"It woulda bin aw reet but I forgit to flap."

YEARS AGO when each dale had its own transport and railway engines were new, a farmer was out with one of his workers who was only fifteen. He was astonished to learn that the lad had never seen a railway train.

"Away with ya to top o' yon hill and bide theer till tha sees a train," he said and directed the lad above the entrance to a tunnel. The lad came back very excited.

"I've sin him an' he wern't half scared."

"Wot does ta mean. Aw dost tha knaw it seed thi?"

"Well, as soon as 'e seed me he let out a shriek and ran into an 'ole."

A VISITOR walking down a street met an old lad hobbling along with two walking sticks. The visitor was sympathetic and said "I'm sure you must get very tired if you walk far."

"Aye, but tha's not going near graveyard is ter?"

"No I'm not – but why?"

"Well I thowt if tha were, tha could get me a fresh pair o' legs." The old man hobbled off with a cheeky grin on his face.

"IT WERE a grand match," said a Yorkshireman as the crowd were leaving Old Trafford after a Roses Match. "It were grand defensive battin' by our lads."

A Lancastrian on hearing this retorted, "It was worst game I've sin i' years."

FOR A LONG life, eat wot thi likes. Drink wot thi likes. Then go off to bed and let the two on 'em feet it aht.

AN ANCIENT clock in a dales village church was famous for its accurate time-keeping. Then a vicar decided to replace the old lad who wound it up with an electric motor. One day the clock failed to strike eleven o'clock. The old man glared at the vicar: "Theer tha is, reverend. I told thee it wouldn't work reet if thi 'ad yon clock electrocuted."

A brave father was showing his young son the view from the cliff top down to the south landing at Flamborough. He was holding the lad by the hand but he was also holding the sandwiches. The mother shouted, "Thee come to me, lad, and if thi father's stopping theer in yon spot, tek t' sandwiches wi' thee."

A YOUNG lad in Leeds spent a holiday at his uncle's farm in the dales. When he returned home he was asked by his parents if he had enjoyed his holiday.

"I enjoyed every minute," he said.

"What did you do?"

"Well mostly I was the lavatory attendant to twelve cows."

A SMALL boy was absent so the teacher asked his slightly older sister the reason. The reply was, "My lile brother 'asn't cum cos 'e hasn't bin, but mother 'as given 'im summat to mek 'im go and when 'e's bin 'e'll cum."

An old lady in Thirsk was sympathising with a friend of her husband who had his leg amputated. "Ee, I's sorry lass — did they tek 'is foot off 'an all?"

A HAPPILY engaged girl was talking to her father about the wedding. She said, "Daddy I want my wedding to be like the music of a great orchestra with violins predominating."

"Nay lass, it'll be more like a band wi' brass predominating."

A CEMETERY keeper and his wife had just moved into a house on site and were busy decorating. He nipped out for a quick pint to introduce himself to the locals.

"Welcome lad – tha's a new un but where's thi wife?"

"She's busy strippin' in t' cemetery."

A DALESMAN visited a new doctor, complaining of a cough.

"Well I would suggest you stop smoking."

"Nay lad, I've tried that dozens o' times an' it's nivver worked."

AN ELDERLY couple in Leeds were showing signs of age and owd John was in bed with the doctor at his side. Owd Mary looked on as the doctor said, "Prepare yourself, lass, he's almost gone."

The old man awoke, glared at the doctor and growled, "Nay, doctor, Ah'm not dun yet."

His wife interrupted, "Thee shut up, John, and listen ter t' doctor. He'll know better than thee."

A YOUNG lass on the North York Moors was asked by her mother to go to the nearby farm to collect the milk. The farmer told her that he could not supply her because a cow had tuberculosis.

The little lass got home and told her mother, "We can't 'ev no milk cos cows gitten two little horses."

A TRAMP knocked at the front door of a doctor's surgery on the outskirts of Bradford. He asked the posh woman who opened the door if she would give him an old pair of the doctor's breeches.

"The doctor does not have any," the woman replied.

"Well can tha gah to him and ask 'im?"

"I can't do that."

"Why can't thi'?"

"Because I am the doctor."

WHEN YOU are gardening how do you tell which are good plants and which are weeds?

"Tha pulls 'em all up. If they grow agin they be weeds."

Bird Nests

Ah've gi'en up burd nestin';
Ah shant tak' the'r eggs
It's noan fair ter t' birds
An ah scrat' all me legs.

Will Clemence

JOHN LIKED his pipe but the vicar did not like the habit. "John," he said, "if the good Lord had intended you to smoke he would have put a chimney in the top of your head."

"Aye," was the reply "and if he'd meant thee to tek snuff he'd 'ave put thi nose t' other way up."

WITH THE coming of the alarm clock the knocker-up became redundant. A knocker-up in Bradford failed in his duties and one chap, late for work, was admonished by the doorman.

"Has thou not git yan o' them alarm clocks?"

"Nay, I's gitten a knocker-up. But if ahr knocker-up can't knock foak better than he's doin' ah sal 'ev to find a knocker-up wot can knock ahr knocker-up up."

A DOCTOR in a Ripon hospital was examining an elderly farmer admitted for severe pains in his back.

"Where do you get the worst pain?" he asked.

"Well," was the reply, "I gits 'em mainly in t' barns when I's mukkin' aht."

A LAD WAS waiting in the market place shivering but eating an ice cream.

"Why ister shivverin'?" asked a local.

"Because this is the fifteenth ice cream I've 'etten and my girl still hasn't turned up."

"Well why don't you get a hot drink?"

"I daren't. We've nivver sin each other. It's all been done by writing. I told her she could tell it were me cos I wud be eatin' an ice cream."

A Big Mouth

An unfortunate man up in Gayle
Dropped his teeth in the beck says the tale;
Now a cow down at Hawes
With the same size in jaws
Has the prettiest smile in the dale.

"THERE'S NOT as many old folks as there used to be," said Ben to his wife as she cleared the table. He took the tablecloth outside to give it a shake when some local children who were playing outside bolted.

"Hey up," shouted one, "t' awd lad's coming."

Ben went indoors and said to his wife. "Ah knaws where all t' owld folk are lass – we're them."

NOTICE outside a farm near Richmond:

"Wanted – Woman to wash, iron and milk three cows."

A CLERK was doing his rounds in Leeds to compile an up-to-date voting list. He knew there were two brothers who were twins and approaching ninety. He knew one had died but was not sure which one to delete. The survivor he knew was stone deaf and he held the book in front of him and shouted at him:

"Which is dead?"

The answer came quickly.

"It's t' other un."

"Aw, c'mon. It's only five mile apiece!"

AT A VILLAGE cricket match the local squire was annoyed to be given out lbw. He stopped on his way back to the pavilion and said to the man in the white coat, "You need glasses, my man, giving me out like that."

"So does thee, mate – I'm nobbut sellin' ice cream."

A DALESMAN employed by the vicar was caught telling a lie and his master said, "Now then my man. One far greater than either of us notices everything we say."

"Ah knaws that, vicar. She's already spoken to me abaht it," as he looked at his wife in the kitchen.

In the First World War an old dalesman was told that the Germans made their uniforms from cloth made from nettles.

"Reet," said old Ned, "why don't we chuck caterpillars at 'em?"

IN A MARKET town near Scarborough a fish merchant was worried that very few people were stopping to look into his shop window. He put a notice up close to a huge fish globe in the window which read: FILLED WITH INVISIBLE GOLDFISH FROM THE ARGENTINE. This drew the largest crowd ever seen in this town.

A BAD-TEMPERED old lady in a Bradford mill area complained during the war of shortages.

"Why 'as thee got no onions? That's nowt to do wi' t' war. It's all dahn to thee."

"Nah, it's not. Onions is wanted fer t' war – they use 'em to mek tear gas."

A SCHOOLMASTER was trying to explain the difference between male, female and neuter. She asked, "Can anyone tell me something which is not feminine, not masculine but is of the neuter gender?"

Up shot a hand and a boy shouted, "A cock ladybird."

A proud but rather pompous city dweller was speaking in the dales and pointed to a medal he had been given for his work by none other than the Queen. An elderly lady looked at it and pointed to it saying, "Ee, that's a grand un. Our Bert has gitten three o' these for playin' darts."

A DALES farmer had just hired a lad. "Wot will I 'ave ter do?" asked the lad.

"Do? Do? Tha'll 'ave to wark. Ah can laik bi missen."

A HOLIDAY group who were visiting Dent thought they would take the rise out of an old roadman who at that time was the Methodist Society steward.

"Why was Dent railway station built so far from the village?" they asked.

The old man replied, "'Appen they wanted it near t' railway."

A THRIFTY shopkeeper who had done well in business decided to open another shop in a neighbouring town, putting in a manager, who was allowed to employ a youth as assistant. Entering the shop one day when the manager was out, he saw a youth leaning on the counter, smoking a cigarette. He said to him, "And how much do they pay thee?"

"Eighteen shillings a week," replied the youth. Handing the youth that amount, he said, "Here's thi wages: now get out."

When the manager returned he said to him, "About that lad of thine, I've sacked him; I'll noan have anybody wasting my time."

"Nay," replied the manager, "that weren't my lad. I nobbut asked him to look after t' shop for a minute while I went out."

THRIFT WAS shown by the village undertaker who married the local midwife, so as "to have 'em both ways" on his sign. This stated: "You may linger, but we'll get you yet."

AN OLD dales farmer was having a quiet drink when the landlord asked him why his hens had all stopped laying.

"Aye, they's all stopped – ivvery one on 'em."

"Why is this?" asked the landlord.

"I's bin 'aving a shippon built. Hens were listening when they 'eard a couple of them workers boasting abaht t' wages they was earning laying bricks."

A SCOTTISH boarder said to his landlady in Yorkshire, "Excuse me, missus, but did you get my name?"

Landlady: "Yes, it's Sandy."

Boarder: "Oh, that's a' richt. Judging by the helping I got I thocht you thocht it was Gandhi."

AN OLD Dales farmer, noted skinflint, was approached by an electrical firm to get the order for wiring his premises.

"How much will it cost?" asked the farmer.

He was quoted a price, but said it was too much. Oil lamps had been good enough for his forebears so he would make do.

Shortly afterwards the old man had a fire and the agent called again.

"Now what about being wired up? Oil can be very dangerous you know."

"'Appen tha's reight," said the farmer, "but when Ah kicked t' lamp ower Ah wor drunk on home-made wine, but it wean't 'appen agean."

"How's that?" enquired the agent.

"Because Ah've teemed t' wine down t' sink, and signed t' pledge."

A DALESMAN rang the door-bell of a posh house and it was answered by a prim housemaid.

"Can I speak to Mr Pennington-Jones?"

"Which one – there's two of them lives here?"

"Tha knaws," was the reply, "the yan wot 'as a brother who has a big mill in Bradford."

A YOUNG Yorkshireman joined the army and was sent to do some fighting abroad. He had never seen a real battle before and at the first crackle of a musket he dodged behind a tree and shouted, "If they carries on like this somebody's baund to be kilt."

His sergeant called to him, "Come on! Be a hero and we shall live in history."

"Nah," was the reply, "I doan't want to live in 'istory. I wants to live i' Pudsey."

An old dalesman, found poking his stick under the front door of his cottage, was asked what he was doing. "Nay dang it," he replied, "Ah've just shoved t' key through't letter box an' forgotten to lock door."

AT A TIME when there was a threat of division in the Cabinet in Victorian times, a Methodist preacher with liberal leanings speaking in Skipton prayed:

"Oh Lord, at this critical junction of events, be pleased to grant that Mr Gladstone and his supporters may hang together."

A well-known Tory shouted, "Amen! Amen!"

The preacher recovered by continuing. "Oh Lord, I mean, may they in accord and concord hang together."

The old Tory retorted with, "Amen! Amen!" and then in a loud whisper added, "Any kind o' cord will do."

THERE WAS a test match at Headingly in the 1930s and it was hot and the scoring was slow. In fact, the day was boring. Suddenly from the street outside a motor bus backfired and the loud report echoed all round the ground. A Yorkshire voice shouted out, "By gowd t' scorer's shot hissen."

Old Lizzie, a widow of a farmer, was far from happy with her milkman. She sent him a note: "Thee send one bottle o' milk and one bottle o' watter and I'll mix me own."

A DALESWOMAN rang the doctor in a panic and said that her young son had swallowed her fountain pen.

"I'm on my way, but what are you doing about it in the meantime?"

The reply was instant: "I'm using one o' them new-fangled ballpoints."

DURING the war an officer passed the time of day with a couple of the cleaners at the camp.

"We've got the fire burnin' a treat," one said, "but could thee ask one of the lads to see to the kennel's fire?"

The confused officer said, "I did not know we had dogs at the camp."

"Nay, we doan't. Not the dogs' room but the kennel's room [colonel]. Tha knaws, 'im wot runs t' camp."

"When I said it would pay for itself, I didn't mean what you mean."

A VERY posh young lady from the south married a York-shire farmer. She did not like the local dialect. She objected to being called 'Mrs Olive Hoyle' and decided to use her husband's name and called herself Mrs Nor-man Hoyle. Ever after she was known as 'Mrs 'En Oil'.

A farmer in Swaledale was asked if he had ever taken a holiday. "Nobbut yance," he said, "that was when t' wife ran off wi' our lodger. But it didn't last long 'cos she soon cum back."

A YORKSHIRE lad got a job which meant he spent half his time in Leeds and half in London. He was asked the difference between the two places. His reply was: "When I go to a Leeds house they put the kettle on – down yonder they take it off."

A farmer was forced by his wife to move and live in a new house. He agreed but only if he could name the bungalow. He called it Costa Plenty.

TO 'CALL' anybody still means in some parts of the West Riding to abuse or to insult. A teacher from the town speaking to a class of six year olds from the dales asked the name of her father. When she looked confused the teacher asked, "What does your mother call him?"

"She doesn't call him nowt. She loves him."

A SHORT sighted chap lost his hat in a gale and chased after it. "Wot's tha doin'?" asked a daleswoman.

"I's after mi 'at."

"Well it's time you stopped chasin' that black un of mine."

TWO LITTLE lasses in Bradford were discussing their piggy banks. "It's daft to save money."

"Aye, it meks folk into misers."

"An' it meks parents into bank robbers."

A COUPLE from the dales were hungry after chasing around Otley Show for hours and so they set off to find food. The old lad pointed to a notice which read 'Dinners from 12 to 2 o'clock'.

"Reet lass – in 'ere, he said. "Two ahrs steady eatin' is nooan so bad for nobbut one-an'-a-tanner."

A VERY shabbily dressed farmer's wife entered a local bank and asked about deposits and interest. The bank manager explained at great length until finally the woman went to the door and called to her husband who came in carrying a heavy bucket.

Upturning this onto the counter, out poured coins and notes of every value. While the couple looked on the manager counted the money. At last he turned to the woman and said, "Well madam, you are just short of a thousand pounds."

The woman glared at her husband and growled "Thou girt cloth 'ead, thou's brooat t' wrong bucket."

> There was a young housewife of Pickering
> Who marred life by her bickering.
> Her husband cried "Jane
> Thy natterin's a bane
> And t' light of my love's nobbut flickering."

A DALES farmer went to a show. "How did you like it?" someone asked. The farmer scratched his head. "Well, if Ah wor goin' agean, I wouldn't go," he said.

A MAN from Leeds around 1900 went into his local grocery and asked for one-pennorth of butter.

"Nay, Bob, I can't mek thi a pennyworth."

"Can tha mek two pennyworth?"

"Aye, I can do that," said the grocer and duly cut it.

Bob looked at it, pulled out his pen knife and cut it in half.

"Nah then, thee tak one hawf and I'll tak t' other. Here's mi penny."

A PEDLAR entered the tap room and was greeted by the landlord. "'Ow do, Jack, it's a lang time sin I saw thee. I thowt thou were dead."

"Aye," replied the old pedlar. "Ah've bin dead a long time but I's too idle to stiffen."

Two mill owners from Bradford were taken by a client to visit York Minster. They looked in awe at what they saw. "It's a reet champion spot is this. Just thee fancy 'ow many looms we could get in 'ere."

A CHOIRMASTER in a dales chapel was rehearsing with his choir and said, "The trebles lead until they come to The Gates of Hell, and then you all come in."

There's a visitor here.
Eeh! Ah hevn't hawf laughed.
He doesn't talk reight;
He says crackers for daft.

He speyks vary funny.
Ah heard him blawt aht,
"I've nothing at all,"
I' steead o' "Ah'm baht!"

He says ears for lugoils.
Nay – not even lugs;
An' then he says carries.
Ah knaw he means lugs.

He doesn't say "Sithee!"
Like other fowk does.
But afore vary long
He'll be talking like us.

Will Clemence

"I HEARS that yon flu epidemic's ovver in a lot o' spots but it's still here tha knaws. It all depends on t' bottle."

"What bottle," asked the old lady's friend.

"Well tha sees ivver sin my Fred found we had a drop o' whisky left ovver from Christmas he's been doin' nowt but try to ward off t' simptums."

OVERHEARD at Headingly during a Roses match. After a good stroke, a man with a posh voice shouted, "Well done that man."

A spectator glared at him. "Art thee frae Lankisher?"

"No."

"Well is you a Yorksher chap?"

"No."

"Then thee mind thi own business."

AN OLD lady had been very ill. When she recovered, some wealthier relatives offered to take her to the seaside for a break. Arriving at the hotel there they were shown into luxurious private apartments.

The old lady went into a doze. Waking up she saw that a maid was setting the table for tea. A beautiful cloth and fine crockery were laid out.

"Turning to the maid, the old lady said, "Hey, lass, tha shouldn't have bothered wi' t' Sunday tea things. T' owd pots woulda done."

A MOTHER told her son to fetch her a turnip from the nearby farmer. "Ask for one bigger than the one we got last week," she said. "Get one as big as your head."

The lad told the farmer what his mother had said. "Get into t' field an' 'elp thissen," said the farmer.

The boy was away about an hour so the farmer went to look for him. He found the lad near a huge pile of turnips and asked, "What's tha doin'?"

"I've tried me cap on 'em all an' it won't fit," the lad replied.

A FELLWALKER entered a Dales inn and got into conversation with a local farmer. "Will you have another one?" asked the walker, after several glasses of ale had been drunk.

"Nay," was the reply. "Ah musn't stop. Ah've t' van outside wi' t' lambs, sheep and t' missus in it."

A daleswoman walked into a chemist shop to buy a thermometer to put in the first aid cupboard. "An' tha can gie mi yon o' them Farrinight things. I'm telt that they're t' best brand."

A YORKSHIRE dentist was asked how men and women reacted when he told them they had to have all their teeth out. He grinned and winked, "Women say 'will I be able to talk?' and men say 'will I be able to eat?'"

Then he said, "But please don't tell my wife."

A DALESMAN who usually walked to the market in Hawes was offered a lift in a car. As the vehicle struggled to get up a hill the old lad asked if it could not go any faster.

"Nah, it's nobbut a seven-horse-power car."

"Ah, then I reckon six on 'em must have deed."

TWO WORKMEN near Pateley Bridge were building a waterwheel. The day was hot and one said, "Let's give ower an' go yam. Rome wasn't builded in a day."

"Ah knaws that," replied the boss, "but I wasn't t' foreman."

"MORE RAIN – more rest," said a new farm hand.

"Wot did thi say?" growled the farmer. The lad thought quickly and said, "More rain – more grass – more milk – more brass."

"Tha'll do well lad," said the farmer.

When folk say that money is the root of all evil they mean that it's about other folk's brass but never their own.

A WOMAN on a Ripon bus sat next to an old farmer. She got out a map of India and began to spread it out. She kept bumping into the farmer who grunted in annoyance. Eventually the farmer reacted and said, "Ey up missus, is tha sure tha's on t' reet bus?"

A SINGLE decker bus was just pulling out of Bingley when a young man rudely pushed his way in. He grinned and said, "Is th' Ark Full?"

"Aye," shouted a wag from the back, "but there's allus room for an ass. So tha can cum in."

Tall Tales

A tall lighthouse keeper from Spurn
Saw the lighthouse collapse with concern
But to full height he rose
Hung the lamp on his nose
And there it continued to burn.

A VICAR was passing a farm when he heard two lads using very bad language. He looked to find the reason for this outburst and discovered that they were trying to load a mule into a cattle lorry.

"Can I help?" asked the vicar.

"Aye, tha can. Seein' tha's a parson tha can show us 'ow Noah got two of 'em into an ark, cos one wain't go for us."

AN OLD dales farmer decided to pay one of his infrequent visits to town to see a relative. Arriving early on the bus route he whiled away the time by having a crack with the local roadman. Presently the bus went flying past without stopping to pick him up. The dalesman shouted and the roadman whistled and the bus ground to a halt. As he crept aboard panting for breath the conductress said, "Ey up, Jack, tha nivver signalled."

"Signalled?" Jack snorted. "There were nae need to signal. Tha shud a knowed Ah needed pickin up when Ah hed mi Sunday cleeas on."

A VERGER in a dales church was found on the floor of the vestry obviously looking for something. The vicar's wife asked if he had lost something.

"Nay, Mrs Reverend, it's thi 'usband. He fell in 'ere last neet and somebody said he'd lost his equilibrium."

DURING the war there was a long queue for the bus and when it was full there was no room for the next man in line. "Nay, let me get on. Ah mun git to mi job. I's part of t' national effort."

The conductress looked at others who were also left behind and retorted, "It'd mek nah difference if tha were part o' t' National Anthem," said the conductress, "we're still full," and she rang the bell.

COMPUTER support team: "What kind of computer do you have?"

Dewsbury man: "It's a white un."

A FARMER'S wife was not pleased at the price she received for her eggs and wrote on one egg: "I got next to nowt for this egg. Wot did thee pay for it?" She added her name and address.

To her surprise she got a reply later than she expected: "My dear Madam. I was recently performing in a music hall in Barnsley and I received your bad egg for nothing."

A HEALTH visitor told a class of children not to fondle animals. She asked a little lass for her comments: "Aye missus, tha's reet. My Auntie Annie used to kiss her dog?"

"What happened next?"

"It deed."

A GRAVE-DIGGER was plying his trade when his spade struck an ancient and uncharted coffin. The lid flew off and the tenant of the coffin popped his head out and the following conversation ensued:

"Nah then young man, is t' Resurrection Day already?"

"Nay lad, tha's too early. 'Ow long aster been in 'ere?"

"Nigh on two hundred year."

"Well nah, wot's it like?"

"Can't grumble ...nobbut unless I had a pint now an aggen."

"Do lads dahn theer still enjoy a sup of ale?"

"Aye they do."

"'Ow much is it a pint?"

"It's a bob."

"Nay, that's too dear. Thee put t' lid on aggen."

A ROAD worker in the dales was noted for his sense of humour. He was asked, "What are you doing these days?"

"Aye lad I'm on wi' a reet big job at present."

"What's that?"

"I'se fed up wi' mendin t' Pennine chain. It's brokken agean i' two spots."

AN MILL owner in a Yorkshire village was known for his meanness and the bullying way he treated his workers. When he died all his workers heaved a sigh of relief as he was buried. The vicar was surprised when he saw that one young lad stood by the grave for a minute or so on his way to work every morning.

"I did not know you were so fond of your old master," remarked the vicar.

"Ah's not," was the reply, "I'm nobbut makin sure he's still theer."

Call to computer helpline: "Good arternoon. My box sez it can't print and sez 'Can't find t' printer'. I've lifted it up and put in reet by the screen but it still sez it can't find it. Mine must be a blind un."

A LITTLE girl wrote in her notebook: "An altercation is the speech wot ends a wedding ceremony."

A FARMER bought himself a new bike but did not like it. He offered it to his mate.

"Nah," was the reply, "its nah use to me."

"But tha can ride it to market. Tha'd look daft tryin' to ride a cow."

"Aye," the mate replied, "but I'd be even dafter trying to milk thi bike."

A dalesman, glowering at his pretty but lazy daughter, said, "Aye she's like York Minster. She looks grand but she don't move much."

OLD BOB was 'not reet bright' and was sent to the village shop by his wife. "Here's a shillin'. Thee gah and get me a pound o' currants."

As he was setting off she called him back, "Thee git me some butter an' all – here's another shilling."

He returned without the shopping and looked confused. When asked what the problem was he said, "I can't remember which shillin' was fer t' butter and which fer t' currants."

"I CAN'T get on t' internet" complained a farmer.

"Are you sure you used the right password?"

"Aye, I saw mi son use 'is."

"What is it then?"

"It's nobbut five dots."

AN ARTIST outside a gallery in Leeds was carrying his portfolio when he stopped to look at a pavement artist who was using his chalks to produce a picture of a ship and a shark. The young artist sniffed and said, "How can you paint a shark when you have never set eyes on one?"

"Don't thee worry, lad," was the reply. "Some of you academy lot paint angels and none of you will ivver see yan."

A criminal wanted by the police was photographed in four different positions and sent to all the Yorkshire towns. The police in York received a phone call from an officer in a small dales town. "It's alreet sir," said a voice at the other end, "we've arrested all four on 'em."

AN OLD West Riding chap sat with his friends in the pub. "I hear old Tom's deed sudden."

"'Ow owd were he?"

"Ninety-five."

"Well then, that's not so sudden."

A POSH couple spotted a tea shop in a dales village, went in and began to see if the place was clean. They were greeted by an old lady in her apron who said, "Nah then. If tha's stopping git thisel plonked."

"I couldn't get a yard dog – but this one's two-feet-eleven!"

A WELL-TO-DO lady had a son attending one of Yorkshire's best public schools. She approached the rugby field and asked one of the lads training there, "Can you tell me if my son the Hon Algernon Swanker is among that crowd?"

A boy looked round and shouted, "Come on, Stinker, your mother's here!"

AT THE END of the village gardening show a fella was walking home with his marrow which had just won first prize.

"I'll give you a shilling for it," said a lady.

"Nay lass, that's not enough. I paid two bob fer it misel."

A vicar found a bottle of cherry brandy on his doorstep but no name was with it. At the end of his sermon he said, "I must thank the anonymous person who sent me some cherries. What pleased me most was the spirit in which it was sent."

AN OLD farmer and his wife were in the market at Leyburn. The owd lad was bothered with toothache and his wife said, "Git thi to t' dentist an' 'ave tha tooth aht."

Off he went to see the dentist whose surgery was kitted out with all the latest equipment.

"Now then my good man," said the spruce young dentist, "where's the offending tooth which I have to take out?"

"Just tek aht first yan tha comes to," said the patient.

The confused dentist asked the farmer to open his mouth and only then did he understand. There was only one tooth left in his mouth.

A FARM LAD from Wensleydale was a witness in a case at the assizes and was cross-examined by a counsel about the size of a certain hoof print left by a cart horse.

"Now tell me, how large were the hoof prints?" asked the counsel.

The lad pondered a bit.

"Nay," said the lad "they was nobbut ordinary 'oofs."

ON OTLEY market day a herbalist was boasting that he had a cure for any complaint. "There's nowt in t' pain line but there's an herb to shift it," he stated.

"Wot's tha gitten for heartache," shouted a wag from the crowd.

"If tha's smitten wi' that there's nowt fer it but thyme," was the quick response.

A SELBY man bought his mother-in-law a plot of land in the cemetery as a Christmas gift. The next year she glared at him, saying, "Why aster got me nowt this Christmas?"

"Because thou hasn't used what I got thi last year yet."

ONE OLD dalesman did not believe in helping out in the home and was half-asleep in his armchair.

"Wot's on t' telly?" his wife asked him.

"Nobbut dust," was the reply.

"I was thinking of going to a cricket match today," said one man to another, "but you know how it is — trying to find a place to park, getting through the crowd to get in, and besides, if it doesn't rain, it may be terribly hot."

"Yes, I know what you mean," replied his friend. "My wife won't let me go either."

"T' milk looked a bit weak so Ah'm puttin' it through agean."

A COUPLE in Bradford were disturbed by a drunk lying under the table of a pub. Seeing the lady blush the chap asked, "Dosta knaw 'im?"

"Aye," she said, "he were my first boyfriend. When I married thee he started drinkin'."

"It's a miracle," he commented. "Fancy going on fer all them years still celebratin'."

A STRANGER to the dales passed a man who was well known as the local poacher. Without knowing this he asked if he knew the best place to fish in the area.

"Aye, I do that," was the reply. "Walk along t' river bank until tha sees a sign wot sez next to a field, 'No Road'. Mek thi way across it to a lile wood wot sez 'Trespassers will be prosecuted'. In t' middle o' that wood tha'll find a tree wi' a notice on it which sez 'Private Fishing'. That's t' best spot for miles."

A WIFE, sitting on the side of the bath naked, said to her husband, "Tha knaws Alf, I look to be getting fat and ugly. Say summat abaht me wot's reet."

"Don't worry, lass – there's nowt wrong wi' thi eye-sight."

TWO Catholic priests decided that they needed to take a break and planned a holiday from the Yorkshire parish. Off they went to Florida and were sitting on the beach wearing the most trendy garments. Their attention was drawn to a lovely young blonde lady who was topless.

"'Ow do, father," she called and passed on.

They were so sure that they had worn something which broke their cover and so they changed into something more garish.

The next day the lady was there and said, "'Ow do agin, father."

One plucked up courage and asked, "How did you know we were priests?"

"Well father," she replied, "I sees thee ivvery week. I'm Sister Benedicta."

A bride-to-be was discussing the pros and cons of marriage. She said, "It's a lile bit like mi mother's rag mats. Tha's got to stick at it till it's finished."

IN THE old days there was a packman who had a round in the Arkengarthdale area. He was always willing to buy rabbit skins. This was in the days when all rabbits belonged to the landlord and a tenant farmer could be turned off, should he be found rabbiting.

However, money was scarce and there was always a good supply of skins, much to the annoyance of the gamekeepers.

One day the packman paid his usual visit to the gamekeeper's house and the latter soon spotted a parcel of skins.

"Tha's gitten a grand lot of skins theer. Who gets 'em for thi?"

The packman leaned closer and said, "Can tha keep a secret?"

"I can that," said the gamekeeper with a gleam in his eye.

"So can I," said the packman "I'll si' thi agin soon."

Two women talking about their husbands: "Aye lass, the less a man knaws, the prouder he is of his knowledge."

A DRAPER'S shop in Leeds was advertising seersucker cloth which was used for dress material. An old countryman came in and said, "I wants yan o' these blood-sucker cloths if there's inny left."

AN ILKLEY man thought nothing of the new bungalows which had just been built next to his old cottage. The builder was trying to get him to buy one; the old lad was not convinced but he went in.

He went into a room on his own and said to the builder, "Canst thou see me?" he asked.

"No."

"Canst thou hear me?"

"Yes, course I can."

"Aye lad tha can't in my 'ouse. Thy walls is too thin."

A LADY from Bradford sent her daughter to buy three pounds of baking apples from the local shopkeeper. When the girl returned, her mother weighed them and set off to the shopkeeper.

"Tha's nobbut sent me two-and-a-half pounds. Tha's cheatin'."

"Nay lass – did tha also weigh yon little lass?"

"MY DAD'S just been to t' dentist and got a new set of teeth," said little Johnny proudly.

His friend looked very interested. "Coo!" he replied, "What are they going to do wi' old ones?"

Johnny looked thoughtful. "I suppose they'll save 'em and cut 'em down for me," he said.

A LITTLE girl had spelt 'tram' correctly and then the teacher asked her, "and what would be left after the T has been taken away?"

"T' dirty cups and saucers, miss," was the reply.

Pockets of conversations overheard at an elderly persons' outing to the Dales:

> *"Ah knaw he's gittin' on a bit. He gits winded playin' dominoes."*

> *"Old Fred allus sits in his rocking chair but he can't mek it rock."*

> *"Aye, these days everything aches – what doesn't ache doesn't work."*

> *"Owd Sally puts her bra on back to front an' she sez it fits better."*

> *"Ah feels better joining a health club, but Ah've no energy to go."*

> *"Ah feels as knackered in t' mornin' after, even if Ah's bin noweer."*

> *"It's not t' pace of life that concerns mi, it's t' sudden stop at t' end."*

> *"Ah'm done wi' wild oats, lass. Now Ah'm into prunes an' All Bran."*

AROUND 1900 a notorious character called Bobbiner used to stand in the middle of Huddersfield blowing a cornet and holding forth his political and religious views both of which were of an extreme nature.

It was known that he had just returned from a visit to a mental institution and somebody shouted out, "Tha's not reet in thi 'ead."

Bobbiner replied in an even louder voice, "'As thee owt to show tha's not daft? I've gitten a ticket to say that I's not barmy no mooer."

An old farmer's wife who was familiar with the industry before mechanisation was remembering the days of her youth. "There's not much real haymecking these days — it's almost allus this salvage stuff."

BEFORE pollution had done its worst, the stream had once held lots of fish. Looking over a bridge on the Aire a little lad looked at an angler and called to him,

"What's tha fishin' fer, mister?"

"Salmon," was the reply.

"Nay, there's no salmon hereabahts."

"Tha's reet, there arn't nah fish at all so I maht as well fish for salmon as owt else."

A TEACHER was struggling to get a young girl to understand grammar. She told her, "You should remember the rhyme, 'It is I said the spider to the fly'."

The girl thought and replied: "Why can't it say, 'It were me, said the spider to the flea'?"

TWO OLD Whitby men were having a chat over a pint. One said, "Wot's ta bin doin' this arternoon, George?"

"Oh, nobbut lookin' for a bit o' jet on t' beach."

"Wot's tha gitten fer it these days?"

"Six shillin' a pahnd."

"Don't sell it yet. Price'll soon be goin' up. They be flyin' aircraft on it nah tha knaws."

Not noted for throwing his money about Eric tackled his wife about her present. "I want summat that will go from nowt to twenty in three seconds," she said.

"Reet," he replied, "I'll get thi a set of bathroom scales."

A MAN visits his solicitor to make a will and asks, "What exactly do I have to do?"

"It's perfectly simple," replies the solicitor. "You answer a few questions then you leave it all to me."

"But," says the client, "I was planning to leave some to my wife."

DURING the First World War the vicar visited an old man living on his lonely farm. The old chap asked, "How's t' war goin' on?"

The vicar told him what he had heard.

"Well they've gitten a fine day for it," he said as he looked at the sun shining out of the window.

"Nah, being a granddad doesn't make me feel old," said the Wolds man to his pal. "It's being married to a grandma!"

DURING the depression between the two wars, a lad got so tired of being on the dole that he decided to ask a fell sheep farmer for a job.

"Does ta think tha can help wi' t'sheep?"

"Aye, Ah can manage owt."

"Well, now, Ah'll gi' thi a trial. Go up t' moor an' bring in t' sheep – all on 'em."

After an hour or two the farmer went down to the fold to see what had happened. There were the sheep all safely gathered in, but with the youth lying down exhausted.

"By gow!" said the farmer, as he looked into the fold, "Tha's done a grand job. But tha's getten a fox among 'em."

"Is there?" wearily replied the lad, "Well, he's geed me more trouble than all t' rest put together."

OLD SARAH was in her garden when the vicar passing said, "Are you having a good day Sarah?"

"Aye, I's pickin' carrots, onions and turnips."

"My word, they all look tempting. You can make a really good dinner without any meat."

"Oh no. I likes a bit o' meat I does. I've gitten a nice lump of beef an' I'll add it to mi camisole. It'll mek it reet tasty, like."

THE DOCTOR asked the farmer's wife, "Did you give your husband the sleeping powder as prescribed?"

"Yes," she replied. "You said I had to give him enough to cover a three-penny piece. I didn't have one, so I used three pennies. But it's all reight, he's still sleeping."

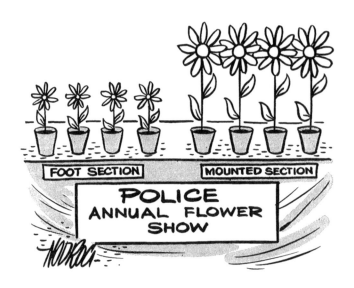